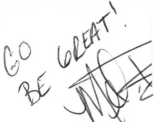
Go
Be Great!

M000303211

CHASING BENTLEYS

THE POWER OF ACCOUNTABILITY IN ACHIEVING YOUR GOALS

Melissa L. Burrow

FINN-PHYLLIS
PRESS

Published by Finn-Phyllis Press, Inc.

Chasing Bentleys / Melissa L. Burrow - 1st ed.

ISBN 978-1-7330337-9-4 (pbk)

ISBN 978-1-7330337-8-7 (eBook)

For Isabella—you teach me every day how to live my best life, and you are my most treasured gift. I know you will make a positive impact on this world.

CONTENTS

W e spend so much of the precious time we have on earth chasing what we want—but so often we do so without an actionable plan. We chase money, success, love, self-worth, goals, and confidence by looking outward, never looking where the power truly is: inside of us. When you decide you want love, success, money, and confidence and you look inward to find those things and bring them to life, you will instantly be on the path to living your best life.

After so many years spent chasing everything I wanted without yielding results, I became accountable to myself and took control of my life. No one is going to make you successful if you haven't made a decision that success is what you want. You can chase all the things you want in life without holding yourself accountable to actionable, strategic steps (and continue to run in circles). Or, you can make the decision today to read this book and change the course of your life.

While everyone is designed for greatness, most don't seek the knowledge or activate the drive necessary to go after what they want. They instead choose to follow the crowd, chasing those things that they believe will make them happy. They chase every "Bentley" they see and are distracted by all the glitter and glam they think will bring them fulfillment. People have asked me why I use a "Bentley" as the metaphor for what each person's heart desires. The answer is simple: I have been in the automotive industry for over twenty years, and in that world, a Bentley represents luxury, class, power, success-all of the things we are taught to chase. Every one of us knows people who link so much of their self-worth on the things they have. I love luxury items, and someday I will buy a Bentley, but not to define or validate my worth. I enjoy the expert craftsmanship and high quality of items, but I look inward to define my worth and seek knowledge over approval. I like to enjoy the fruits of my hard work and success, and material things mean little to me in the big picture of life, but to be able to drive in comfort and experience the quality craftsmanship of such an exquisite automobile would serve as a reminder that strategic actions yield results. It (like my vision board) would be a visual reminder of my successfully applied principles of accountability and strategic action.

Unfortunately, hard work has diminished so many people's lives instead of enhancing them. We see them working their lives away, building wealth for corporations and companies who make them feel guilty for taking hard-earned vacation time. We see them living their entire lives regretting opportunities they choose not to take. When they retire, they will likely either be too tired to travel or too ill to enjoy the retirement that they worked for their entire lives. And that is, in the end, their choice. They choose to look outward instead of inward to take the actionable steps necessary to live a limitless life.

The fact is, you can choose to live your life "on the sidelines" or you can open your mind, digest the following principles, and take the next step. The ten years I spent reading everything I could get my hands on in order to empower myself was invaluable, but I certainly could have continued to simply follow and applaud. I could have continued chasing. Or, I could have chosen the more difficult but rewarding path of learning and implementing. I chose the latter.

Too many people don't advocate for themselves. They waste time and energy waiting for validation from someone or something to make them happy. All the while, the most precious commodity we have (time) is going by. Moments, days, and years are wasted. The truth is, we each hold the key to our own happiness and fulfillment. No one else has it. As a single woman and mother who absolutely knows her worth, the concept of settling to statistically appease the cultural standards society imposes on us as little girls, to follow the status quo, goes against everything I believe in. There is a stigma surrounding the label "single mother" that tends to elicit comments such as, "You really should have tried harder in your marriage" or "I am so sorry he left you." Anyone who has uttered those words is wrong. I told my husband to leave. It was my decision, and it was the best decision I could have made for my daughter and myself. I no longer had respect for my husband; he had broken a vow in such a way that it could not be repaired. He is a wonderful father, but he was a terrible husband. Today, we are great co-parents and friends.

I know many women who feel the same way I did and decided to live their best life without settling. The women I know who are happily married or happily single are focused on living their best life, and are not interested in having anyone in it who isn't like minded.

What society or others think about your personal decisions should have no bearing on your life. You are in control of the decisions you make, and you have to be willing to be accountable to those choices. When you become accountable and make choices for yourself that speak to your desires and purpose, you start to embrace change and develop the inner strength required to take actionable steps.

This book shares the "magic" that happens when you let go of fear, embrace accountability, and take control of your own life. If you are reading this, I want you to know that I care. I care about you, and I understand. My life has been far from perfect, but I want to take you on this journey with me. I want you to be a part of my story. I want you to start actively being aware that you are the author of your own story. I want you to know that you are valuable, worthy, and special. The people you have allowed to be in your life are there by your choice. If you have people in your life who are not supportive or do not bring value to your life, I hope to encourage you to respectfully remove them. I have mastered the technique of "loving people from afar," and doing so has greatly improved my life.

I have a secret to tell you: you can achieve any level of greatness you desire.

What if fear and low accountability are the only things holding you back? What if YOU are your only obstacle? What if you took control of your circumstances and changed your life?

If you are someone who blames and complains, I implore you to stop and have an open mind—even if only for the duration of this book. It is an open mind that allows transformational change to occur. This book is for wolves, not sheep. I will challenge you to rise up and be the change in both your company and life. I will challenge you to call out friends who complain about their circumstances but are not willing to put in the work to change them. I will challenge you to know your worth and never apologize for your success.

I wrote this book hoping to make a positive impact by sharing my story and journey thus far. I wrote it for people who know they were meant to do more, be more, live more. I wrote with the hope that my story and my experiences can help others. I want you to truly know that you are one decision away from living the life you want. You are the only person who has the power to make that happen. I want success for you, but that isn't enough. You have to want it more than anything else in your life. You have to want to change and embrace personal growth. You have to put your ego to the side and listen to mentors and coaches. You have to be willing to invest in yourself. Everyone is chasing something. Whatever your "Bentley" is, make sure it's what you truly want, and then take accountability and create actionable steps to get the result you desire. Stopping and putting together an actual plan makes far more sense than constantly running in circles but going nowhere. I'm here to hold your hand through the journey.

At this point in my automotive career, I am a thought leader and industry expert. I have embraced the destination to which my path has led me, and I have opened myself up to infinite possibilities along the way. I stay true to my vision, I embrace change, and I am constantly evolving. I take every opportunity to educate myself and focus on personal growth as much as professional growth. I'm passionate about helping others to see that they have the ability to transform themselves and live a life that is far from ordinary. I am an accountability coach, and simply put, I want everyone to find their own version of happiness.

Ultimately, the dreams you chase are the ones that will shape your life. It's time to stop merely chasing and finally reach your dreams through intentional action.

CHAPTER ONE

THE POWER OF ACCOUNTABILITY

The first time I attempted to write a book, it was a work of fiction. I was eighteen years old, and *Chasing Bentleys* was, ironically, the title. The story was about a group of friends who individually struggled with one of the seven deadly sins. Also known as the capital vices or cardinal sins, these sins include pride, greed, lust, envy, gluttony, wrath, and sloth, and they run contrary to the seven virtues. Each character struggled with an inability to exhibit self-control over their specific sin. If I do say so, the character development was amazing. I had such a passion for each character and crafted each of them with meticulous detail and different levels of emotional intelligence. While each was tempted by the vices that the others struggled with, they fell victim to their own deepest inner struggle.

This group of friends went through their lives unaware therefore unable to address obstacles that were holding them back. I also created characters who represented each of the cardinal virtues of prudence, justice, temperance, courage, faith, hope, and charity so that they could interact with the others and offer up opportunities for them to learn and grow into the people they were meant to become. The characters who were challenged by the capital vices of pride, greed, lust, envy, gluttony, wrath, and sloth resisted change; only one of them was able to change, evolve, and shift into a life where she could be more, do more, and live more. She started pursuing true happiness and was passionate about finding her purpose. She became a person who was accountable to her goals. She was humble, and she educated herself on how to achieve success and grow, not only professionally but personally.

She was and became...me.

I never published that work (except as a short story in a college magazine). As a young girl, I dreamed of being a famous author on the *New York Times* bestseller list. As much as I wanted to become a writer, I hadn't learned how to hold myself accountable to my goals and dreams and had no idea the power I had inside me to make my dreams a reality. I didn't know what life coaches, business coaches, or most importantly accountability coaches were, so instead of following those dreams, I went into the male-dominated automotive industry, in which I have had great success for more than twenty years. I love this industry, and I have met so many amazing, talented people throughout my career. I always wanted to return to writing, but the universe had other lessons for me to learn before it would give me back the undeniable urge to write the book you're holding in your hands.

It's important that I define the word accountability so that we are all on the same page. New Oxford American Dictionary defines accountability as "the fact or condition of being accountable; responsibility."

I went through a period of life in my late twenties and early thirties when I felt lost. I struggled with feelings of depression and the sense that I couldn't isolate my greater purpose. I began to read every personal development book that I could get my hands on and loaded my toolbox with motivation. While I became inspired, I had no idea where to go from there. I decided that I needed to dive deeper and really look at why I wasn't satisfied with my life. I started asking myself the tough questions and continued to stumble on the same concept required to truly move forward in life: accountability. I researched what accountability was and became enthralled with both the concept and the results of implementing it. Accountability not only fostered clarity in one's personal life but by becoming more accountable, one's professional capabilities improved as well. This was the most promising research that I had come across and once I fully embraced the concept, I fell in love with the effect it had on my life and found purpose and passion in teaching others about its power. I found joy in helping people by holding them accountable and watching their goals become their reality. I know that my journey, like yours, might not be what I had envisioned for my life at each point along the path, but the lessons that I have learned and the education that I have received have brought me to where I am today, walking in my purpose: as a mom, an executive, and an accountability coach.

Embracing accountability helped me transition from a scared eighteen-year-old girl to a powerful woman with focused goals and a plan to explore what happiness truly felt like...for me. We each have our own "happy," and right now, at this moment (and for every moment hereafter), I am committed to living in this space. Kindness, humility, accountability, confidence, and empathy are all pathways to happiness. You may be reading this and thinking that you are not looking to achieve massive corporate success. In fact, you might not have a passion for a career of any kind, but I can guarantee that you want to feel your version of happiness. We all do.

My hope is to encourage you to honor and take accountability for every aspect of your life the good and the not-so-good.

You must take responsibility for your own life. It isn't anyone else's responsibility to make you happy. This world owes you nothing. You get back the energy that you put out. When you commit to being accountable, you change your own life. After my own accountability epiphany, I began to study the power of accountability further, including the way it empowers us to create actionable plans to achieve our goals. I discovered that accountability has two distinct benefits.

The first is helping you to isolate and identify your life's purpose. Do you recognize what makes you happy and how that activity or principle is integrated into your life? When you recognize the gifts that you have been given and the way they relate to your purpose, becoming accountable will only further clarify and magnify that purpose.

The second benefit is that, when your purpose is defined and your skill set is sharpened, you are more able to stay accountable to actionable steps. This is achievable by self-disciplined creators or those who hire accountability coaches to get them (and keep them) on track. Staying focused on your goals and holding yourself accountable (or having someone else hold you accountable) is one of the greatest investments that you can make in yourself and your happiness.

I was so impressed with the changes that personal accountability made in my own life that an unexpected life purpose of my own became clear in the process. After immersing myself in extensive research in and around accountability, I started to engage in accountability coaching. It has been amazing to witness the positive transformations that have resulted. I feel so grateful and privileged to contribute to my clients' personal journeys in order to help them achieve their goals.

There are so many wonderful coaches who inspire and motivate. There are also great business coaches. But after all that coaching, you need someone to hold you accountable as you walk through actual actionable steps to maximize your potential for greatness and live in your purpose. Once you've worked with an executive coach or business coach to help you write out a business plan, what comes next? Can you hold yourself accountable amidst all the world's distractions, or will your motivation fade without a consistent accountability checkup? I firmly believe that everyone can benefit in some way from working with an accountability coach, either as a short-term insurance policy to get your purpose off the ground and implement structured action, or as a partner you can work with for a specific length of time to keep distractions at bay and focus on whatever it is that you're struggling to make a priority.

I look at accountability as three distinct phases, and I'll discuss each of these phases as the book goes on. The first phase includes those who just removed the past they've been carrying around. The second phase is stepping off the tightrope. The third is taking actionable steps that can be implemented into daily life. Once one has committed to and gone through each phase, they can start to actively live in their purpose and design a life that will bring them joy and happiness. But in order to be successful in reaching your goals, you need to be consistently accountable in the areas discussed in this book.

Accountability Acrobats

I want to talk for a moment about a quality that I've seen time and time again, and one that you need to be on the lookout for in yourself as you go through this process. Saying that you're willing to be accountable and actually being it are two different things. Excuses are the go-to response for people to whom I respectfully refer to as Accountability Acrobats. A common approach that demonstrates zero actual accountability is saying something along the lines of:

I am so unhappy, but it is not my fault because I have had zero help in my life, and I didn't grow up with the advantages that others have. Life is unfair, and I am stuck in a pattern of debt. I am stuck in a dead-end career. I have had so many bad things happen to me, and others simply will never understand because I had a bad childhood.

The first clue that a slew of excuses may be on the horizon is the statement "I am unhappy." Excuse number one may be "I didn't have the advantages that others had." Excuse number two is perhaps "I'm stuck because of debt." And excuse number three often involves blaming the past (a bad childhood, perhaps). By making those statements, one is doomed to be stuck in a vicious pattern, always blaming others for the life they don't have. To turn this belief into a statement of accountability, rewrite the narrative to one such as this:

I have created a plan to pay off my debt because, in the past, I have mismanaged my finances. I am actively looking for career opportunities in positive environments where I am able to learn and grow professionally. I prioritize and choose happiness for myself and grow from the experiences I have had in my past. I am choosing to live a purposeful life full of gratitude and opportunity.

Do you see the difference? People who do not take responsibility for their actions confine themselves to the restraints of the blame game. They are too busy pointing the finger to work on themselves and truly live the life they were meant to live. If you are not living with accountability, you are living in shackles and chains that are binding you to the belief that you are nothing more than the by-product of a series of circumstances.

ACCOUNTABILITY STEP

The first step to accountability is gratitude. List five things you are grateful for. Find meaning in your gratitude, and if you're having trouble getting motivated to start a big project, start by connecting its completion to some good in the world or to people who will be impacted by it. Having gratitude is good. Practicing gratitude will lead you into accountability.

CHAPTER TWO

THE PANIC BUTTON

O ut of nowhere, your heart begins to race, your breath quickens, your palms are sweaty, nausea sweeps over your body, and you are afraid you may pass out. Thoughts start racing through your head, telling you that everyone is noticing your distress, you are going to lose consciousness, perhaps you are having a heart attack. Panic sets in; your body takes over. You succumb to the fact that the shallow breathing and panic sweeping your body must be a heart attack, and now that you have diagnosed yourself, your arm begins to tingle and you are not sure if you should run or call 911 for an ambulance. You start thinking about what you need to do, that you can't be ill right now, and then *What if, What if, What if...*

There is a reason that I'm inserting this topic early on. For one thing, panic is a natural reaction to the idea of making a major change in one's life. For another, the workaholic tendencies that many of us take on can have disastrous consequences. Knowing that you aren't alone if you've experienced any level of intermittent or ongoing anxiety as a result of working too hard is important not only to validate your experience but also to encourage you to adopt new habits. You can be successful and panic-free.

I have always been extremely ambitious, striving to be the best at whatever I am doing, and early in my career, I had a tendency to take on too many projects. I felt compelled to master the skills required for whatever position I was in by working the hardest, reading as many books as I could on the subject, and overworking myself to prove that women could be just as successful as men in the automotive industry. I believed that if I worked harder than everyone else, I would establish myself as the industry leader I knew I wanted to be. I was the first to arrive at work and the last to leave. In my spare time, I did everything I could think of to learn how to be as effective as I could be at my job while providing the highest level of customer service.

The outcome of my overachieving tendencies was that I pushed my body and mind to the point that I'd created a stress-filled environment that had serious health consequences. I'd work straight through lunch and didn't devote any time to relaxing or working out. I was in my twenties, and I felt invincible. I worked fourteen-hour days, six days a week, and still went out with my friends at night, limiting me to five or fewer hours of sleep per day. I lived this nonstop lifestyle for years. I took no time off work, never went on vacations, and truly thought that my success hinged on my ability to outwork every single one of my coworkers.

In my experience, the biggest challenge in male-dominated industries comes from the "boys' club" mentality. I was not invited to their weekend golf outings and rarely to their nights at the bar (and when I was, I declined in order to keep the rumor mill silent). I knew that I'd only get my shot climbing the ladder by outworking everyone else. It's one thing to say that there is a glass ceiling for women, but it's an added challenge when you are also dealing with a boys' club into which you don't fit because you're a woman. It creates a tough work dynamic, and it added to the stress that came with my desire to prove my worth by taking on any and all projects that I was asked to take on.

I always thought that anxiety was something that "weak minded" people experienced. I never dreamed that I would experience it myself. But the nonstop lifestyle that I had embraced and that I thought was so valuable, if not completely necessary, in advancing my career was actually beginning to cause a biological stopping point to protect my body from further harm.

There I was, living life, working my normal six days a week, when I was asked to handle a software conversion that would require that I be at the store on Sundays for a few weeks so that the installation team could work while the store was closed. As usual, I jumped at the opportunity and agreed to oversee the conversion on my only day off. It was the end of the month, which, in the auto industry, is one of the most stressful times because everyone is working to ensure that they hit their monthly goals.

I was a finance director with several finance managers working underneath me, and I thought that I could get a head start on close-out by being there on a Sunday. The Saturday before was brutally busy. I got to work around 7:00am but didn't leave until 11:00pm. I was too busy to eat lunch, and after work I met up with my boyfriend to listen to some live music nearby my apartment. I went to bed at about 1:00am and set my alarm for 6:00am so I could get back to the store. This was my life and maintaining this kind of schedule was completely normal for me at the time. I had no idea what meditation or gratitude lists or breathing techniques were. I only knew that I was going to create my own success at any cost.

When my alarm went off, I bounced out of bed, took a shower, grabbed my dog (ironically named Bentley), and headed to my office to wait on the installation team.

I first drove to Starbucks and ordered my usual: a triple shot venti cinnamon dolce latte. The day started out just like so many others, but little did I know what would soon happen and how it would change the way I lived my life from that point forward. I unlocked the side door and settled into my office to dive into work. I worked for a few hours before starting the coffee maker in my office so that I could drown myself in even more caffeine.

I received a call from the installation team that they had arrived, and I let them into the area where they needed to work. I was a few more cups of coffee in to my day when I started to feel a little "off." I got up and made my way into the ladies' room, where I began to feel even more off kilter. Suddenly my heart started to race. I looked in the mirror, and I was pale. I felt dizzy and began to think, "Ohmigod, I am the only one here besides the outside team of people working on the computers. What is going on?" I made my way out of the bathroom and back into my office, trying to stay out of sight. Once arriving back to my office, I could no longer stand, so I sat on the floor of my office with hands shaking. All I could think was, "I'm dying."

I suddenly realized that I couldn't breathe and started gasping for air. At that point, I was really scared. I crawled over to my phone and called to ask one of the other managers to come to the store. I told him that I was really sick and needed to leave, but the installation team was there. My co-worker reluctantly agreed, shocked that I was asking for help. This was the first time in my life that my mortality hit me in the face and the first time that I had experienced a total lack of control over something. I immediately dialed my best friend and asked her to drive to the store as well after convincing her that I was having a heart attack and needed to go the ER. Short of breath with my heart racing, I knew I couldn't drive myself. Both my friend and my co-worker arrived, and they were both shocked by my state.

I was only twenty-five years old, too young to be having a heart attack for heaven's sake. I wondered, If I die who is going to take care of Bentley? Who is going to do close-out at work if I am not there? Tomorrow is Monday; I simply can't have a heart attack today!

My friend walked me to her car and sped to the ER. They immediately rushed me back and hooked me up to monitors. They administered some medication, and I quickly started to feel better. I thanked the nurses for saving my life and asked them if it was normal for a woman in her twenties to have a heart attack. They cautiously nodded and smiled, then let me know that the doctor would be right in.

The doctor came in and told me something that I didn't expect to hear: I was perfectly healthy. I hadn't had a heart attack. In fact, my tests all came back normal. That news is, under normal circumstances, great. But when you have just suffered the biological symptoms of a heart attack, fear starts to set in.

The doctor calmly explained that what I had experienced included all the symptoms of a panic attack. He asked me about my stress levels, my diet, and my exercise regimen. He asked me about my caffeine consumption and how much sleep I was getting. He referred me to a doctor who later performed a stress test on my heart just to make sure that the initial findings were correct. What had happened to me was nothing more than the result of the collective abuse I had put my body through for years finally manifesting itself.

When the ER doctor initially suggested that what had happened to me was a byproduct of anxiety, I completely shut him down. I didn't have anxiety. I was a strong person! He patted me on the arm, looked me dead in the eye, and said something I will never forget.

"Young lady," he said, "You have one life to live and one body to do it in. I recommend that you reexamine your priorities and start taking care of your body. Remove yourself from high stress environments or pay the physical price. If you keep living your life the way you are living it, you will continue to experience these symptoms. Or, you can take steps to change your life. It's your choice. I am going to write down a name of a doctor who can help you restore balance in your life. Please call her."

That profound experience changed the course of my life and helped me to establish more balance in it. I learned to set boundaries and make my health a priority. If my body had not sent me that warning, I might have ended up actually having a heart attack or worse. Your body can only put up with so much abuse before it will biologically do what it needs to do to protect itself from further harm. I now understand that stress releases hormones that can damage every part of our bodies. When stress sets off the usual ferocious communication between the hypothalamus and the pituitary gland, the signal stops at the adrenal glands. They manufacture and release the true stress hormones—dopamine, epinephrine (also known as adrenaline), norepinephrine (noradrenaline), and most significantly, cortisol. That relaxing walk on the beach (or whatever else you do to relax) that you take time for actually sends signals to the brain that counteract the effects of the abundance of stress hormones.

Over the years, I have learned subtle tricks and coping mechanisms that allow me to handle my anxiety in a healthier manner. Some of the most effective strategies I use are to put both feet on the ground, breathe in and out of my nose, take a walk, be aware of triggers, and live in a positive environment with positive people. Meditation is extremely effective in controlling stress and keeping anxiety at bay. Exercise is another great way to burn off stress and keep your body strong, properly positioned to fight off anxiety and stress. Eat clean and be in tune with your body. When you start feeling run down, rest! This can be extremely hard to do, but it's a necessity to keep your mindset strong and anxious feelings at bay.

While I was resistant at first to talk publicly about my struggles with anxiety, I've found that the more I talk about it, the more I find that other people relate and have had similar experiences. The more responsibilities we take on as we ramp up professionally, the greater the risk that we will begin to neglect our health and wellness routines. That neglect can affect not only our mindset but also our long-term health. When constant stress starts to take over your life, it can manifest in dangerous ways, such as increased anxiety. Stress is a major factor in everyone's health and learning how to cope with it will not only give you better quality of life but will also keep you from suffering from the consequences that come from not controlling it. A demanding career without boundaries, overextending ourselves, and not taking care of our physical health will have a physical price. You are in control of your work/life balance, and only you have the ability to change its course if it becomes out of sync.

ACCOUNTABILITY STEP

- Practice mindfulness every day to ease trigger situations that make you feel anxious.
- Use grounding techniques to keep yourself in the present moment by using your five senses.
- When you are focused on the moment, your brain cannot worry about the future.
- Write down situations, environments, or people that create feelings of anxiousness. Next to each trigger that you wrote down, journal about different ways you can de-escalate your emotional response to help with the automatic biological reaction. Remember, you are in control of your body when you control your emotion.

CHAPTER 3

ABANDON THE TIGHTROPE

Have you ever thought about all of the responsibilities you have in life and considered how amazing it is that you handle everything that life throws at you? You and I are balancing life every day. We juggle all of our to-dos along with dreams of everything that we want to become. But, are we unnecessarily placing ourselves on a tightrope?

You bet we are.

We're trying to be responsible while juggling bills, children, a significant other, time, work, time, time, time, and...in case you didn't hear it the first four times...time. We invite stress into our lives, and we roll out the red carpet for structured chaos and negative thought patterns. Almost everyone finds themselves on that tightrope at one point or another, and I most certainly have been guilty of walking that rope myself before truly embracing accountability.

We the people of the tightrope have our balancing stick in our hands to show everyone that our life is perfect and balanced, and we are winning. We are responsible, and our pictures on social media prove it! We pile our past on top of our back and drag it onto the rope with us, wearing the weight like an invisible backpack filled with lead. We hold our balance stick and very carefully put one foot in front of the other. We slowly walk the never-ending tightrope with our past dragging us down and a glorious smile on our face for the world to see. We can handle it all.

When one is operating in this manner, they believe that their life is the way it is because of their parents, their past, situations that happened to them, or grief they have experienced, but it is never their fault, so on the tightrope they stay. They are the product of their environment, and they have settled for the idea that this way of life is all that there will ever be. They are not successful, because other people never gave them the opportunity. They are not happy because of the hands that life has dealt them. They lack a defined purpose. They are unable to choose happiness because of this or that person or event. Life is unfair and unjust and full of despair and stress. They were cheated out of the life they deserved, and they harbor anger and resentment toward God, other people, or themselves. They bobble on that tightrope, clenching the balance stick tighter and tighter, as their muscles squeeze and their knuckles whiten. And they simply march on, one foot in front of the other.

The music eventually starts playing more and more slowly, transitioning from the cheerful circus tunes of your youth to a sad, slow melody reminiscent of songs written for slasher movies or tragedies. The metaphorical backpack gets heavier and heavier, the years pass, and the lights dim more and more each day until the music finally just stops, and you are left sad, alone, surrounded by darkness, filled with regret, and afraid to jump off of the rope. So, there you stand, in the quiet, watching everyone below choose happiness. And in that moment, you have chosen to live life merely as a spectator. You become a voyeur instead of a participant. Your life becomes a scrapbook of other people's vacation pictures and adventures instead of those you're living yourself.

Accountability is a funny thing. It is necessary to embrace it if we truly want to absorb the knowledge and achieve the growth we desire as we travel through the spectacular experiences that life has to offer us, but it is a tough pill to swallow for some. It will force you out of your comfort zone and into a space of raw uncomfortable authenticity. It can be extremely difficult to shift your mindset to one of accountability if you have not first isolated and identified your purpose. I am definitely jumping ahead of myself, so let's start first with a plan to get you (and keep you) off that rope.

First, and most importantly, you are not your past, and you are not a product of your environment. Put your lead filled backpack down and have a good cry, then prepare to move forward. The past is gone. You cannot change it, nor can you live inside of it. I recommend not even unpacking the backpack you carry your past around in; simply set it on fire. The past is no measure of who you can be now. This step may sound easy, but for some, it's the hardest one to take. After all, you have carried around the past for your entire adult life, and it has become a part of what you perceive to be your identity. You only know yourself as a product of your past, and leaving that behind is terrifying.

It is okay to be scared and feel lost at the thought of redefining your existence so that you can live a life of purpose filled with joy. But doing so is not only recommended, it is necessary to your redefinition of self so that you can get rid of the weight you've been carrying around. You must find comfort that once you truly get rid of whatever is weighing you down, you will discover and clearly see who you are meant to be. You will be inspired to go on a journey of self-discovery and redefine who you are and how you feel.

If you do not choose to let go of the past, you are subscribing to a life filled with health problems that are a direct result of the unnecessary extra weight you are carrying. Emotional illness (anxiety, depression) and physical illness are some of the risks you are taking a chance on by carrying around that heavy reminder of it. That backpack can get so heavy and large that you begin to shrink in comparison to it, to the point where all that is visible to you and others is your past. If this happens, the past will slowly take over your life and become not only the past but the present and future as well.

Now, inside that backpack may be some trauma. Let me stress that, in this instance, taking accountability is not the same as admitting that things are your fault. I am going to explain the difference so that it's clear that I do not lack empathy, and I am in no way suggesting that you are to blame for any traumatic experiences in your past. Allow me to demonstrate.

An example of powerfully framing your experience is saying, "I am accountable for swimming in my grief and living in my past over the past five years and missing out on living my best life, however it was not my fault that the tragedy or negative situation happened."

We can only be accountable for ourselves and our feelings, so if another person has inflicted trauma or brought grief into our lives, their choices and actions are out of our control. We can only hold ourselves accountable to our response to events. The way we respond to the things that happen to us or around us is what we need to be willing to be accountable for.

We make choices every day that impact the world around us as well as our own circumstances. We can choose to make changes, or we can choose to complain. We can keep walking the tightrope and piling on the stress until we become physically exhausted and ill, or we can make the decision to start living our best life.

If you are still reading, I commend you. You are on the path to change, grow, and live your best life. The people who have put down this book and dismissed it are, perhaps subconsciously, afraid. Fear of the unknown is a strong motivator, and if we cannot accept that we are the reason that our lives are the way that they are, we are doomed never to reach our full potential and, instead, become a spectator in our own life.

After shedding the past, the next step to accountability is confidently stepping off the tightrope. When I set down my own backpack and dropped the balance stick that I had faithfully used to keep from falling, I had one of the greatest revelations of my life: my eyes had been closed the entire time. I was concentrating so hard on carrying my lead-filled backpack and balancing with the help of the balance stick (and smiling while doing it) that I never stopped to open my eyes and really look at the world around me. The tightrope that I had been walking on so carefully so as not to slip and fall was not two hundred feet in the air, the way I'd always pictured it in my mind.

It had always been on the ground.

With eyes wide open and the heaviness of my past removed, I stepped to the side and into the sun. I knew that I alone was responsible for the unhappiness that I had experienced in my past because I stayed on that tightrope. I was afraid to step off; I was afraid to fall. When I decided that I was no longer afraid and not going to allow anyone else to control my future, I stopped blaming and complaining. That was the moment my eyes were fully opened.

ACCOUNTABILITY STEP

Work-life balance may seem impossible to fully realize but you can blend the two with great results. Start by eliminating anything that is wasting your time and not producing results. Who can you delegate responsibilities to in your life that will help you achieve a better balance?

CHAPTER 4

ELIMINATE PEOPLE PLEASING

My mother was a stay-at-home parent until my parents divorced when I was thirteen. From that point on, I was raised mostly by my grandmother and received a postcard when I was eighteen announcing that my mother had remarried in Las Vegas. My mother was never what I would call a "happy person," and she never really found her purpose. She was someone who constantly blamed others for her situation, unable to take responsibility for her circumstances.

She was plagued by various illnesses and was not one to place any sort of emphasis on achieving happiness or eliminating fear from her life. It is now clear that she not only lacked purpose but also settled for being an unhappy person, destined to live an average life. I am confident that many of the illnesses that she suffered were a direct result of her anxious, unhappy nature. With a change in diet and exercise as well as an identified purpose, I would like to think that she could have experienced more joy in her lifetime.

My father, who always dreamed of becoming the next great entrepreneur, was in construction. He was a natural leader and people were drawn to his charisma, which allowed him to move up in his company quickly. As a result, moving to different cities where his job sites were located became normal. I moved around so much as a child that I can't tell you what elementary school I attended because every six months I was in a different school. While this wasn't ideal, it did give me the opportunity to develop strong communication techniques that would allow me to become a good listener and authentically connect with other people.

I have very few memories with my parents of the silliness that I exhibit now with my own daughter and even fewer memories of trips to museums, parks, zoos, and normal weekend outings that many people remember as a child. Our home was not filled with laughter and joy but instead an air of merely existing. I have no idea what my parents' passions were or what they enjoyed doing. I don't know that they did either. I know that we never talked about things like purpose and gratitude the way I do with my own child.

It took a long time for me to learn to understand and embrace the value of the experiences I had growing up. Without those experiences, I would not be where I am today or have the ability to understand and communicate with other people who did not grow up in a stereotypically healthy environment. The definition of a positive environment is definitely open to perception and varies greatly for different people and diverse personalities. I choose to look at my time as a child as a unique opportunity to develop a specific set of skills that benefited me later in life. I choose *not* to live in a prison of my past, and I'm grateful for the lessons I learned.

I knew, even as a child, that the life I was going to live was not going to be anything like the one that my parents lived. I remember being seven or eight years old and deciding that when I grew up, I was going to live a life full of purpose and happiness.

My childhood and the need of acceptance that I craved as a child did present itself as an approval addiction that, until self-diagnosed, caused me to limit myself. That approval addiction was the illuminated pathway by which I unknowingly invited negative energy into my life. Those who understand the desire to please (or at least not disappoint) understand the label of "people pleaser." The people-pleaser monster that lives inside each of us can cause us to almost demand approval with sometimes disastrous results. Regardless of your current situation, if you break your approval addiction and stop being a people-pleaser, empower yourself to embrace the power of words (which I'll talk more about in a bit), and practice accountability, you will see a huge difference in not only the quality of your personal life but also your professional life.

We all naturally seek acknowledgement and recognition for a job well done, but approval addiction is something entirely different. It can leave us enslaved to the notion that we are not good enough unless others tell us that we are. Giving this power to others takes power away from our own innate energy. If you are waiting for someone to pat you on the back or tell you how great you are, you are limiting yourself as well as the energy that you are putting into the world. You cannot tap into your full potential until you get rid of the need for constant approval.

If receiving constructive criticism ruins your day, it's likely that you suffer from an approval addiction. When your employer gives you constructive criticism, how do you respond? Do you say, "I'm so sorry, I will do better" or "Thank you for the feedback. I appreciate your perspective!"

If "I'm sorry" is consistently the beginning of your response, you are not properly utilizing the feedback. You are so addicted to trying to please everyone that you cannot even process valuable tips that may actually help the situation. This puts you in a victim's state of mind, while the second option empowers you to process the feedback and apply it if value is present.

When you read the second of the above two possible responses, how do you feel? The positive energy associated with this option gives you a completely different feeling than the other. If you are reading this and thinking, "That is just not reality," I challenge you to call a friend and ask her if she will listen to two different statements and tell you which she prefers as a response. Everyone responds more powerfully to positive statements.

An endless need to seek approval can also be seen in the practice of comparison. Anytime you compare yourself to others, it's a signal that you are looking for approval. When you find yourself spending too much time on social media, scrolling through endless photos of people you have never met in person and comparing your life to theirs, you need to think logically about what you are actually seeing. Why are you comparing yourself to anyone? When you are simply concentrating on being the best person you can be, you have no time for comparison.

Social media should be a fun way to connect with other people, not a competition. I am a huge fan of social media as a means to connect with people without geographical restrictions, and I choose to use social media to spread positivity into a world that is sadly getting further and further away from frequent face-to-face interactions. We as a society are becoming more isolated and, as a result, less happy. If you are unable to identify the value in scrolling through your feed, take a break from social media altogether. It should be a platform that allows you to connect with people in a positive way. When you post a picture and obsessively check your post to see how much engagement you are getting, it's an indication that you are seeking approval and engaging in people-pleasing behaviors. I am certainly not suggesting that you shouldn't care whether or not you get engagement on a post, but if your mood depends on it, it's a clear sign that your emotional investment may be more destructive than it is valuable. If, at any time, social media is taking away from you being able to live in the moment or affecting your sense of well-being in the "real world," pay attention to the amount of time you are spending scrolling and consider cutting way back.

You do not need approval to be who you are. You are not a victim of your circumstances. The past is the past, and it does not exist in this moment. We have to realize that all we are guaranteed is the moment that we are in right now. As you are reading this, know that you are uniquely designed to achieve the level of happiness that you want. The choice is yours: will you be defined by your circumstance or rise above and reinvent yourself to live the life you were designed to live?

We all need to shed the need to please people. It is an unnecessary narrative to our path, and it will only distract all of us from our goals. The way I changed my behavior and was able to stop craving the approval of others was through the incorporation of three simple habits.

Affirm It!

Affirmations program your brain to make you receptive to change. "I am" statements train your brain in terms of how you see your reflection. That's it. In simple terms, positive sentences build up self-belief in the subconscious mind.

For thirty days, right when you wake up, remind yourself that "Happiness is my choice." Every day, look into the mirror, take a deep breath, and say those four words with conviction. That affirmation will start your journey of self-empowerment. You will notice a difference very quickly, but it is important that you continue to do it for the full thirty days. When the thirty days are complete, you will have established, in your subconscious, that your happiness is not governed by other people. It exists only within yourself. I used to hear the saying "You have to love yourself before you can love anyone else" and not believe that by simply loving yourself, positive people who also love themselves would be drawn into your life. I was incredibly wrong. If you have not established that YOU are going to control your own happiness, your happiness will always be dictated by the approval of others.

Many research studies address the power of positive affirmations, noting specifically the neurotransmitters that are affected by them. The brain uses neurotransmitters to communicate information continuously, and affirmations seem to set positive pathways for these brain travelers. The research indicates that beliefs are not only thoughts we hold but actual brain mechanisms mixed with emotions. The input our brain takes in from the environment goes through a filtering process as it travels across one or more synapses. Eventually, information reaches an area of higher processing, such as the frontal lobe. This is what we think of as conscious awareness. However, the portion of our sensory information reaches these higher levels is, to some degree, determined by our beliefs. Essentially, we can create a more positive belief system by inputting more positive thoughts.

A study published in *Social Cognitive and Affective Neuroscience* was able to capture the effect of affirmations using an MRI. Participants who spoke positive self-affirmations showed increased activity in various parts of the prefrontal cortex and other areas of the brain. Moreover, participants with greater stimulation in those sections of the brain which control processing and valuation exhibited less sedentary behavior afterward than participants who did not speak positive self-affirmations. This research indicates that future behavior as well as thoughts can be improved by positive affirmations.

It's empowering to realize that even when we feel stuck in our emotions, there is a biochemical potential for positive change and growth. When we repeat a positive intention, we become open to pieces of sensory information that we'd previously been blocking with a negative belief. This becomes a self-reinforcing pattern of thought, belief, and behavior. But with positive affirmations, science shows we can change those patterns.

The benefits of positive affirmations are endless. They can improve our self-confidence and ability to overcome obstacles. Positive self-talk also allows us to positively impact the way our bodies feel and biologically operate. One thing I have incorporated into my weekly routine is a mirror technique anyone can do by using Post-it notes or—my favorite—a tube of red lipstick. I pick one positive affirmation a week that I want to focus on, and I put it (or write it) on my mirror so I am forced to look at it every time I brush my teeth, fix my hair, and apply my makeup. I audibly speak it each time I see it. This technique is extremely effective; after a week, the affirmation on my mirror has become programmed into my brain. This technique will give you the following results:

- You will start feeling more comfortable in your own skin
- You will accept the way you look and behave
- Your communication skills will improve
- Each time you do the exercise, you'll give yourself a self-esteem and a motivation boost
- You'll be more positive
- You'll start believing in your own abilities and thus be ready to try new stuff
- You won't feel inferior to others any longer
- You'll appreciate yourself for who you are and will embrace your good qualities
- You won't be afraid to look people in the eye
- You'll appear more confident in front of others
- You'll have a higher opinion of yourself
- You won't have doubts
- You'll be more decisive
- You'll set higher goals and will be more confident in your ability to reach them
- You'll look and be stronger, and people will start treating you differently

What makes the mirror technique unique and practical is the combined power of the mirror, the effect that speaking positive affirmations out loud has on our mindset, and the benefits of doing such a profound activity every single day. It's a mixture of hypnosis, psychology, pep talk, gratitude, positive thinking, focused thoughts, and strong belief.

Harness the Power of No

At their core, people pleasers lack confidence. They worry about the way others will view them when they say no. People don't want to be seen as lazy, uncaring, or selfish, and they fear they'll be disliked and cut from the group, whether it's friends, family, or co-workers.

The power of the word "no" and the empowerment that follows once you start using it will change your life. I was not someone who used that word unless it was backed up with an excuse to ensure that no one could or would show disapproval of the choice I made to decline their request. I would agree to help friends, volunteer at my daughter's school, or build a custom spreadsheet, all while working a full-time job and operating as a single mother. I had a hard time using the word "no" because I didn't want to disappoint anyone, and I wanted to prove that I was a dedicated employee who worked hard. I didn't understand at the time that I felt responsible for everyone else's feelings. The amount of stress that I invited into my life by not harnessing the power of "no" was ridiculous.

If your life is anything like mine was, you commit to too many projects with an already maxed out schedule. You start to feel anxious and tired. You begin to feel unfulfilled and unsatisfied with what your life has become. The routine of your life starts to become monotonous and predictable, leaving little room to explore your passions and interests. You therefore start taking on more and more projects, hoping to become inspired. Instead, you begin drowning.

Saying no is uncomfortable. We've all experienced the anxious feeling one gets after reluctantly saying yes, all the while hearing our gut screaming "No way!" Whether subconsciously or not, we often say yes to things we'd rather not do out of a desire to please. We don't want to disappoint anyone, and saying yes is far easier and satisfying—in the short-term. But long-term, it can leave you stressed out, unhappy, and overbooked.

If you really don't want to do it, saying yes to something can end up making you angry. And, whether you're mad at the situation, mad at the person who asked you to do it, or mad at yourself for agreeing to do it—it's not worth the negative emotion created by doing it.

There is no shame in saying no. You need to get rid of the feeling that you need to substantiate or validate your no. You don't owe anyone an explanation or an excuse. You may fear that your reasons aren't good enough or valid enough, so you end up giving in. But, at the end of the day, if you can't or don't want to do something, regardless of the reasoning, that's your choice and that's all the reason you need.

Trust your intuition and conscience to guide you into deciding if the request is even worth a yes. Remember, your time is such a precious asset, and you need to choose wisely in terms of on what and with whom you spend it. When you are brave enough to say no, the value of your yes goes up. Saying yes *means* something. It's no longer just a passive answer. Even if a "maybe" is the best you can do, you've at least given yourself some time to put more thought into the decision.

"Choose discomfort over resentment."
—*Dr. Brené Brown*

Have you ever stretched yourself so thin just to please other people and gain approval that it feels like you are living for everyone *but* yourself? If you have even once--or are like me and have been guilty of it more times than you can count—I'd like to invite you to take part in a little experiment. The next time someone asks you to do a favor that you know will add stress to your day or interfere with the schedule you have in place, I want you to say no. If you do not teach yourself to say no, you will continue to live in a chaotic state that invites unnecessary stress, all based off a desire to please. The feeling of empowerment that the word no can unleash is so powerful that I urge you to put it into full rotation in your vocabulary. Use it wisely, use it frequently, and use it unapologetically.

Stop Apologizing

Speaking of acting unapologetically, the last step in breaking the chains that bind us to approval addiction is a big one: STOP APOLOGIZING. Saying "I am sorry" has become so ingrained in our speech patterns, and I remember catching myself apologizing for anything and everything. I would apologize for apologizing, and not even second-guess what was coming out of my mouth. I never realized the effect it was having on me. I am not saying you should never apologize. In fact, I am a fan of apologizing when it is appropriate. But not excessively. An example of excessive apologizing is saying, "Excuse me, I am so sorry, but I need you to move your shopping cart over so I can get down the aisle," after which you proceed to move your cart down the aisle and whisper with a smile, "So sorry again, thank you," just to be polite. Polite is saying, "Excuse me, may I move your cart? Thank you." Do you recognize the difference? Learn to recognize it, and stop apologizing for every action.

While apologizing can be a powerful tool for building trust and improving social cohesion, it's vital to be able to assert yourself and view yourself as having the right to make your way in the world. If you're constantly apologizing, you're sending the signal to the universe that you are meek, unsure, and undeserving. An unnecessary "I'm sorry" has huge potential to undermine your power to manifest.

There seems to be a recurring theme of insecurity and low self-esteem that catapults people into (or further into) people-pleaser tendencies. When you actually learn to control your need for affirmation from other people, a world of empowerment will open up to you. If you think about the concept of people pleasing the way I do, you can clearly start to understand that it is little more than a form of servitude that enslaves you to others rather than fostering the genuine relationships and bonds that cultivate healthy relationships. Seeking approval from others is draining, diminishing, and invariably disappointing.

It is draining because you use up so much energy seeking approval that you can't focus on what's really important to you. It is diminishing because your needs often end up dismissed. Disappointment happens because no matter how hard you try, some people are never going to like, appreciate, or value your opinion.

If you find yourself living your life to accommodate others or chasing pursuits just to fit in or gain acceptance, it's time to stop. Though it may initially feel warm and fuzzy to win another's favor, reflect on whether it's worth it in the long run. If you do decide to say yes to others' wants, make sure they fit into your time schedule and are, at least partially, on your terms. Rather than taking on tasks simply to please another, aim toward living by the rules that make sense to you.

What many people pleasers don't realize is that people pleasing comes with serious risks. Not only does it put a lot of pressure and stress on you, it can make you sick from taking on too many things. If you're overcommitted, you probably get less sleep while getting more anxious and upset. Just a lack of sleep and increased anxiety in your life can leave anyone mentally and physically exhausted.

Get rid of the guilt that results from not doing what someone else wanted you to do. The act of self-forgiveness changes the energy and the physical structure of your cells and your DNA. Guilt is a very powerful and deadening emotion, and it can close down the energy systems of your body, thereby lessening the flow of healing energy and love for ourselves and others. Lack of forgiveness is both emotionally and physically damaging.

Sometimes, the most difficult person to forgive is the one you face in the mirror. Some common situations that challenge self-forgiveness include overwhelming guilt from a failed marriage, parenting errors, family and relationship mistakes, and poor financial decisions. Forgiveness is mandatory to fully embracing accountability.

Getting rid of the fear of offending others and the guilt that comes with it will set you free to explore the best way to become a person who embraces growth. In no way am I suggesting that you aim to be a self-centered, egotistical person. Being a generous, giving person is an admirable quality. But accommodating others just to win their approval or to prove your worthiness is another matter entirely.

Start giving yourself the approval that you seek from others!

We live in a world where we are constantly hearing, "Work harder! Faster! Better!" Though this is troubling for many, it's particularly tough for a people-pleaser who thrives off of the approval of others because approval seekers are prone to assuming an abundance of responsibility. If you combine taking on the responsibility of other people's opinions and do not have any tolerance for disappointing others, life can easily become unfulfilling.

Remember, always treat yourself with respect. Know your worth. Value your time. Make choices that are right for you. Instead of feeling pressured to go along with something you don't want to do, speak up. Give yourself the kindness, acceptance, and approval that you're seeking from others.

"To find yourself, think for yourself."
—*Socrates*

"Trust yourself. Create the kind of self that you will be happy to live with all your life. Make the most of yourself by fanning the tiny, inner sparks of possibility into flames of achievement."
—*Golda Meir*

"Once we believe in ourselves, we can risk curiosity, wonder, spontaneous delight, or any experience that reveals the human spirit."
—*E.E. Cummings*

ACCOUNTABILITY STEP

Success is all about falling down and getting back up. How have you overcome a near miss in your past to produce future gains? Journal three positive qualities that you possess and how those qualities help you achieve success.

CHAPTER 5

WORDS HOLD POWER

L et's dive a little deeper into the power of words. Now that you have the tools to break those people-pleaser habits and conquer your approval addiction, it is time to talk about an approach that has drastically altered my life. I am going to say this as simply as I can: WORDS HAVE POWER! I wish I could shout this statement from rooftops all over the world. I am literally bursting with excitement at the mere thought of someone reading this right now and implementing these techniques into their life. Your life will change, your thoughts will change, and the way you physically feel will change. I am going to break this down into two categories: self-talk and mindful word selection.

Self-talk

To start off, let's talk about one of the most destructive things you can do with regard to your mental and physical health: negative self-talk. Negative self-talk will hold you back from achieving success, not only professionally but personally. The more negative things you say to yourself, the more your subconscious will be trained to believe them. Some examples of negative self-talk are:

"I am so stupid! I can't believe I did that!"

"I always mess up! Why can't I be on time?"

"I can't do it!"

"I am just not good enough!"

Never allow these thoughts to set up shop on your brain's highway. Unfortunately, negative self-talk is a learned behavior that can become a physiological response your brain produces in response to a fear of rejection. Doubting our abilities or worrying about how we are perceived lays the groundwork for negative self-talk, so when these thoughts go through your head, you must stop them and apply the label. Question the thought right after you think it and remind yourself that what you've thought isn't true at all. I am writing this hoping that no one reading it says the above phrases out loud. Please, do not ever put these statements out into the world.

One way to evict these thoughts from your mind completely is to start your day with a gratitude list.

Take a blank sheet of paper and write down ten things that you are grateful for. Focus on the positives in your life, not the negatives. Learn to start appreciating and loving yourself. Speak kindly to others and yourself. So many people are loving to everyone but themselves and are their own worst critic. Don't be your own worst enemy.

So many people self-sabotage. There are a million ways we do this, but some of the most common are procrastination, self-medication, stress eating, and interpersonal conflict. Actions such as these are especially insidious because they're relatively small—just one argument, just one trip to the fridge, just one glass of wine—and, in the moment, they may even seem helpful. Self-saboteurs create a vortex of drama inside and around their lives.

People self-sabotage for a variety of reasons. The most common is that they feel as though they don't deserve to be successful. Ironically, many saboteurs work hard and aim high because they're trying to make up for their sense of inadequacy. But when their hard work and high standards lead to good things— material reward, status, or power—they start to self-sabotage and end up imploding.

The reason this happens is a little-known concept known as cognitive dissonance. Basically, people like to be consistent. Our actions usually line up with our beliefs and values. When they don't, we get uncomfortable and try to line them up again. That's why, if we start to stack up some achievements but subconsciously believe that we're worthless, incapable, or deficient, we will (subconsciously) kickstart a plan to ruin it. It feels bad to fail, but not as bad as it feels to succeed for someone who is a self-saboteur. It feels better to control your failure than let it blindside you. When the possibility of failure is something you can't handle, it's easier to take matters into your own hands. Self-sabotage isn't pretty, but it's a dignified alternative to spinning out of control or publicly freaking out. At least when you're the one lighting the match to set yourself on fire, going down in flames is less emotionally painful than having had someone else inflict the disappointment.

As the stakes get higher and you take on more responsibility at work or do something that raises your public profile—you feel you only have further to fall. You believe that if you call attention to yourself by being successful, it's more likely that you'll be called out as a fraud. Some people care more about the image and perception that others have of them, so they completely disregard their own opinion of themselves.

Once in a while, we self-sabotage simply to push buttons. We pick a fight or incite drama to get a rush. This isn't random, of course, because we do all things for a reason. The actual practice of sabotage re-creates a familiar feeling of instability and chaos, plus, if we're stuck at the bottom, we might as well wield some power while we're there, right?

For all of the self-saboteurs out there, do you want to know why you do it? It boils down to the root of everything that holds you back from achieving your success: FEAR.

You likely have a huge fear of failure. Most people think of self-sabotage as fear of success. But deep down, fear of success isn't truly a fear of making it big and becoming a success. It's a fear of trying one's best and not succeeding, of being publicly humiliated. The sheer risk of public humiliation is what creates the greatest prospect of fear. It's enough to make you take refuge by throwing yourself into distraction mode on any form of social media that will carry you out of our life and into the lives of others.

The root of self-sabotage is not knowing how to control your inner dialogue. Using positive self-talk to control your own actions will help break the cycle. Positive self-talk includes the affirmations that we touched on in chapter two. If this is something you struggle with, start writing down three things you like about yourself every day. Read out loud what you wrote every day for thirty days, and train your mind to accept them as reality.

Try using the following positive affirmations:

"I am smart."

"I am beautiful/handsome."

"I am strong."

"I am capable."

"I know who I am, and I am enough."

"I choose to be present in all that I do."

"I choose to think thoughts that are productive."

"I share my happiness with those around me."

"My body is my vehicle in life; I choose to fill it with goodness."

"I feel energetic."

"My life is beautiful."

"I am confident."

"I always observe before reacting."

"I know with time and effort I can achieve anything."

"I love challenges and what I learn from overcoming them."

"I will achieve my goals and the level of success that I want."

This internal dialogue frames our reactions to life and its circumstances. One of the ways to recognize, promote, and sustain optimism, hope, and joy is to intentionally fill our thoughts with positive self-talk. Positive self-talk is about recognizing the truth, in situations and in yourself. One of the fundamental truths is that you will make mistakes. To expect perfection in yourself or anyone else is unrealistic. To expect no difficulties in life, whether through your own actions or sheer circumstances, is also unrealistic.

When negative events or mistakes happen, positive self-talk seeks to bring the positive out of the negative to help you do better or simply keep moving forward. The practice of positive self-talk is often the process that allows you to discover the obscured optimism, hope, and joy in any given situation.

Too often, the pattern of self-talk we've developed is negative. We remember the negative things we were told as children by our parents, siblings, or teachers. We remember the negative reactions from other children that diminished how we felt about ourselves. Throughout the years, these messages have played over and over in our minds, fueling our feelings of anger, fear, guilt, and hopelessness.

Great examples of utilizing positive self-talk

You have a big presentation to give, and the night before you have trouble falling asleep. You wake up exhausted, and you are starting to have doubts that your presentation will be received well. Immediately declare to yourself that your presentation is great, that you are prepared and ready to deliver the information clearly. I take it a step further and tell myself, while I am getting ready, that I am a great communicator. I declare that I will connect with everyone in the room and bring positive energy into the environment. I am capable, I am smart, and I am a thought leader in my industry. I am prepared. I have the power to bring about positive change in the world, and I will do it. I am beautiful, I am confident, I am powerful, and I will not allow negative energy to invade my space.

Those convictions are how I put my mind into a space to be effective. When you start to change the way you speak to yourself, it feels uncomfortable. It is very important that you do not just say the words but actually *mean* them. If this is hard for you at first, start with something simple. Take one negative thing you say to yourself and change it.

Example: "I need to lose weight! I am so fat!"

Change this statement to: "I am going to lose the weight that keeps me from feeling healthy. I am strong."

Complaining about how you look and focusing on your own flaws only reinforces in your brain that those things are true. Changing the way you speak to yourself will allow you to start making changes in your life. It is important that you identify external negative factors in your life that may be holding your thoughts hostage. For instance, your mental state can become toxic by being around friends who are negative. If you are not vigilant enough, you will start to adopt their thoughts as your own. Hence, be alert to what your negative influences are. If they come from certain friends, limit your exposure to them as much as you can. Refrain from discussing your plans with people who will be unsupportive of your dreams and goals and instead surround yourself with the thoughts and actions of people who will empower you.

From uninspired and unmotivated, you will begin feeling uplifted and driven to greater self-growth. The positive energy that these friends vibrate will start affecting the self-talk that you engage in as well.

We have to train our subconscious mind to accept the change before we can put together an action plan to make it happen. At the basic molecular level, we have to put our mind into a position to help our body process the change. The brain translates what it sees and hears into emotions, and it's constantly using context clues and your own words to paint a picture for you. Take control of how your brain is telling you to feel and be very of careful how you speak to yourself. That small voice inside your head can determine your level of success and happiness if you allow it. Retrain that voice to be your advocate and biggest supporter, and watch as the way you feel about yourself changes.

Mindful Word Selection

On to one of the most exciting discoveries I have made on my personal journey of self-growth and awareness. Mindful word selection is very important to shape your future.

I want you to think about someone you know who is a classic complainer. I am not talking about the occasional "bad day rant" that we all can be guilty of out of frustration, but a true *the sun is shining too bright* or *the rain is raining too hard* complainer. Another classic example is, *I just got a promotion, but now I am going to have to work all the time and be away from my family* or *I didn't get the promotion, so now my life is ruined.* Now that you have that acquaintance or friend in your mind, tell me how you feel about them. Are you going to spend all your free time with this person? Why or why not? If you read the previous statements and said to yourself, "This is me," go to the mirror right now, look into it and repeat after me...*What am I doing?*

I am going to share with you one of the most powerful things I have done that has altered the course of my life. Words hold so much power that they can make things happen. I know what you are thinking right now (after you rolled your eyes), but hear me out. I am going to give you an example, a real-life example, of the POWER OF WORDS. Many years ago, before I knew the power of words and the importance of word selection, I would say things without any thought of the repercussions. I can clearly remember turning off my alarm one morning, even though I had a meeting scheduled at the office. I forgot to reset my alarm, and when the meeting was about to start, I received a call from my boss asking me where on earth I was and whether I was on my way. I have always had an excellent imagination coupled with creative energy, so off the cuff, I went into an elaborately detailed excuse (that was absolutely not true). I detailed the specifics of how I was on my way, but my electric garage door opener wouldn't work so I tried the button on the wall, but it didn't work, so I finally climbed up and tried to use the emergency pull, but it had broken off. I took it even further and described how it broke off in my hand and how frustrated I was with the entire situation. I described to him how I could not get my car out, but as soon as the repair person showed up, I would be on my way. I apologized profusely and knew that I had sold the story hook, line, and sinker. I hung up the phone, took a shower, got ready, and even stopped at Starbucks on the way for coffee. I didn't give it another thought. The day passed, the week passed, and a few weeks later something happened that changed my life.

I had made it a priority to be more organized and had been getting up early for work. I had been looking forward to a weekend getaway with my friends for almost a year and had taken a Friday and Saturday off (in the automotive industry, fifteen years ago, it was almost impossible to get your employer to give you a Saturday off) in preparation for my once a year "vacation." I was so excited! I had packed my suitcase and had been calling my friends all morning, talking about how much fun we were going to have in the Bahamas. I had saved my money and bought the plane ticket, prepaid my room, and could taste the mimosa I couldn't wait to order. This trip was the reward for my hard work, and I could not wait to get it going. The day arrived, and I sprang out of bed early, got ready, made some coffee, and with pure glee started packing the car. I called everyone to let them know that I was about to head to the airport. I skipped out the back door into the garage, hit the garage door remote in my car, and...nothing. I jumped out, still with a joyful bounce, and hit the opener mounted to the wall. Nothing happened. Still blissfully unaware, I stood on the door sill of the driver's side of my car and yanked on the emergency release. *Snap.* The rope broke. Now, let me explain that the rope only allows you to be able to pull the garage door down, but I didn't know that at the time. I frantically ran to the door and started trying to pull it up to no avail. I started to panic, realizing that I couldn't get my car out of the garage.

Let me stop the story here and properly set the stage. There was no Uber or Lyft yet, and calling a taxi was not only something you had to pre-plan and schedule but something I wasn't sure how to do.

I was still standing in the garage when my flip phone rang. My cell phone back then was a pink Razor. The flip phone was the most popular phone on the market and the priciest piece of technology that I owned before I got really fancy and invested in a Blackberry. I immediately recognized the number as the dealership that I worked for, and my boss asked me why I wasn't at work. I start explaining that I had requested off several months prior, and that I was trying to get to the airport for my vacation, but my car was stuck in the garage. I went on and on telling the story, explaining that I was panicked and running late.

Then it hit me like a ton of bricks.

My mind started racing while I faintly heard my boss tell me he had already heard that excuse; maybe I was just not the right fit for the store. He suggested that I come by and get my things when I got back from vacation. I just stood there, thoughts racing, faintly hearing the words coming out of my boss's mouth as I relived the exact nightmare I had used as an excuse. I was frozen. In complete shock. The lie that I had made up came true exactly as I had told it. I made it happen. I told a story in detail, and word for word, it happened. It happened *exactly* as I had described a few weeks earlier. How could that be possible? I felt like I was in some sort of twilight zone. I hung up the phone and took a breath. Why did this happen? What in the world was going on?

I missed my flight that day and ended up having to call an installation tech to come over and try to repair my garage door. He couldn't fix it and told me I needed to replace it. He disabled the motion detector that had malfunctioned, locked the garage door in place, and manually opened it for me. He then gave me the price quote and left. I had to call my friends and tell them I missed my flight and would catch a flight the next day.

That one experience caused me to look back on my life and recognize similar things that I had experienced. I was a little scared, but I knew, from that point forward, that I wasn't ever going to lie to anyone again. Years passed, but I never forgot about that experience. You might label it as "God teaching me a valuable lesson" or the universe giving me back what I put into it; I like to look at it as all of the above.

There were many other things that happened over the years that illustrated the power of words in my own life. I would have to write multiple books to go through them all, but I wanted to give you an example to inspire you to think before you speak.

I Speak Life. If you think before you speak and choose your words as if they have the power that they do, your life has the potential to be filled with happiness. If you knew for a fact that everything that you said could come true, would you think before you spoke? Would you choose your words more carefully or, when your emotions are high, would you sabotage yourself and others because of your lack of self-restraint? The decision is yours, and one of the most valuable things that I have learned to do is think before I speak.

For example, how does it feel when you are so angry that you say something you immediately regret? Why do you regret it? If it is just a word, and words hold no power, why exactly are you so filled with remorse? I can tell you why. It's because your immediate reaction is your body responding to the negative energy you pushed out of your mouth and into the world.

Do you think manifestations work? Have you tried them? I can tell you without doubt that not only do they work, if you do your best to only speak positivity into the world, the positive energy will come back to you ten times over. Watch what you say, carefully choose your words, and shut your mouth if you have nothing nice to say. Those three things will keep your eyes on the prize and you closer to reinventing yourself as someone who will achieve your goals.

Still don't believe me? Just look at people who constantly spew hate, complain, and blame everyone else for their problems, and I will show you people who have an unhappy life drenched in the stitch of drama; people not living purposeful lives. I can almost guarantee that their lives are filled with regret and sadness.

Stop the madness by watching your mouth. When you get into the habit of speaking life and stop using words that blame and complain, your energy will shift, and other people who have a similar energy will be drawn to you. Simply put, positive people are drawn to other positive people. Successful people are drawn to other successful people. We will talk about that more in a few chapters, but first, I want you to walk with me into a subject that I struggled with for a long time. You may struggle with it too, or you may not. When I learned to manage my time wisely, all aspects of my life improved dramatically. In the next chapter, we will discuss why time management is important and how improving your time management skills can help you maximize your daily routines.

ACCOUNTABILITY STEP

Are you using a victim's vocabulary or are your words empowering others? Write down one statement you made yesterday that could have been stated differently to positively impact someone else.

CHAPTER SIX

MANAGE YOUR TIME WISELY

I t has been said that the spirit is willing, but the flesh is weak. We know the things that we ought to do, but we don't do them. We know the things that we should not do, but we do them anyway. So, what is going on? My list of things that I want to do and habits that I want to form grows every day, and I find myself eager to get things done. There is nothing I love more than checking things off my to-do list. The key lies in not allowing yourself to become distracted to the point where you don't make changes that will lead to your success. Here are four ways that you can catapult yourself out of the world of distraction in order to get things done.

Isolate the Distractions
Determine what the distraction truly is (turn off your phone, tv, computer).

Create a List of Importance
Write down only what has to be done that day.

Give Yourself Breaks
Stepping away from your project to rehydrate or get fresh air will make you more productive.

Celebrate Your Wins
Crossing items off your to-do list each day is worthy of celebration.

There are so many opportunities in our lives and so many things to try. If you want to stay competitive in any market, expand your knowledge, never stop developing as a person, and keep evolving. You can find a new hobby, read professional literature, set foot in something new, or simply communicate with successful people. These ideas work well if your goal is to become a better version of you.

When you let go of fear, become accountable, and make sure your surroundings align with your vision, your future will become limitless. The positive energy that will naturally radiate from your core will infiltrate every aspect of your life, and beauty will be everywhere you look. You will not feel anxious or depressed, and you will be excited by what the future holds for you.

When asked what surprised him most about humanity, the Dalai Lama said, "Man. Because he sacrifices his health in order to make money. Then he sacrifices money to recuperate his health. And then he is so anxious about the future that he does not enjoy the present; the result being that he does not live in the present or in the future; he lives as if he is never going to die, and then dies having never really lived."

The most precious asset we have in this life is time. Whatever circumstances you have faced, you have a choice to allow those circumstances to teach you something new or to permanently define who you are. Choose wisely. We all know deep down that we are wired for greatness, so why do we continue to live day after day not creating our dreams or making time for our passions? Why do we doubt our abilities just because someone doesn't believe in us? Why do we wait until the time is right? Why do we continue to work for companies that make us feel inferior or invalid instead of worthy and valuable?

We each only have limited time on this planet. How will you spend yours?

If you're not managing your time well, there's no way you're going to reach your goals at work or in your life outside of it. Sure, you might make some progress. But your time management will be an uphill battle if you don't take your time seriously. People who squander and waste the precious little time they *do* have know all too well how difficult achieving even mildly difficult goals can be.

The truth is that time is the greatest equalizer in life. No matter who you are no matter your age, income, gender, race, or religion—you have the same amount of time as the next person. Whether you're filthy rich or dirt poor, the amount of time you have in a day is the same. Therefore, it's not about how much time you have. It's about how effectively you manage it.

Part of the key to time management is simply staying in charge. Here's what usually happens: we start something and we're in control of it, but as the day starts to unfold, we start losing that control. It's like running a business. If you don't stay on top of things, the business will run you before long. You have to stop every once in a while, and ask, "Wait! Who's in charge here?

Here's a good phrase to remember: "Some will master, and some will serve." That's the nature of life, and you have to make sure you become the master. You have to run the day. You have to stay in charge.

The key to staying in charge is having your written set of goals with you at all times. Prioritize those goals, and decide which are most important. Constantly review them, then make them part of a written, weekly game plan.

With your game plan in hand, try to separate the majors from the minors, the really important things from the things that just have to get done. A little thought will save you a lot of time. Ask yourself each morning, "Is this a major day or a minor day? Adjust your time accordingly. Ask, "Is this a major conversation or a minor conversation?" A lot of people don't do well in this area, and the reason is that they major in minor things. They spend too much time on things that don't count and too little time on things that need to count more.

Balance is key. If you lack balance in your life, you're going to feel stressed out. Even if you're able to effectively juggle your responsibilities, without proper balance you're going to eventually reach your breaking point. So, it's important to not only follow a system that will help you get things done, but also one where you prioritize personal and family time.

Don't forget to do things like taking a walk in the park or just sitting and listening to your favorite music with headphones on, or painting a picture, or going on a date night. Those activities are more important than you might imagine. And, when you do them, you achieve a semblance of balance. Because life is short, you don't want to avoid these activities while you're reaching for bigger goals.

Your success should bring you pleasure. Appreciating what you've done and acquired and who you've become is a critical component of fueling your future achievements. Just knowing that you finished everything you set out to accomplish in the day is encouraging! It's these little daily gains that continue to fuel your continued achievement.

Let's say that the evening has come, and you're figuring out tomorrow's game plan. Tomorrow looks pretty light. So, all you write down for tomorrow is "cleanup day." Clean up all the little notes on your desk. Write all the thank-you notes you haven't gotten around to writing all week. Take care of the phone calls that keep getting shuffled from one day to the next. It's minor stuff, but that minor stuff will continue to weigh you down until you get it done.

Even though you spend that next day in cleanup mode—filing notes, writing thank-you cards, making the phone calls at the end of it you will feel like you've accomplished so much, simply because you've taken care of so many little details. It's the little details that can make a major difference.

Little achievements are just as important as big achievements. Success is the constant process of working toward your goals, little achievement by little achievement. Little achievements produce big results.

Expectations set by others should not influence or supersede expectations that you set for yourself. You and you alone will decide what your life looks like, who is in it and, ultimately, what you accomplish. Trust your instincts to know what is right for you and utilize the twenty-four hours that you have.

ACCOUNTABILITY STEP

List five things you accomplished yesterday. Now identify one unproductive task you took on. Your time management relies on identifying unproductive or distracting tasks and eliminating them from your daily routines.

CHAPTER SEVEN

HAVE AN INNER-CIRCLE AUDIT PARTY

You have put in the work and started living your best life, but you still aren't getting the results you want or achieving your goals.

So, it's time to throw an Inner-Circle Audit Party.

Successful and deeply happy people have friends who bring unique perspectives to the table. These friends may employ different habits and live different kinds of lives, but they help grow and expand both your creativity and your perspective. Successful people spend a lot less time talking and a lot more time doing. They aren't as concerned with the perception of being seen as successful as they are worried about getting time to do the work they know needs to get done.

People we are friends with are not always good for us. Sometimes, people come into our lives to teach us something and/or learn something from us. They stay for a season, and then they must leave. Your inner circle of your friends are those people with whom you speak regularly. They are the people you spend time with and with whom you connect. They are the first to know when you get a promotion or celebrate any milestone. They are your best supporters, and they happily applaud your success. They push you and motivate you to do better and be better. They rally around you when they sense you need support, and they offer a safety net so that you're not afraid to jump. Am I correctly describing the people in your inner circle?

In my past, I had the unfortunate experience of getting into a relationship with someone who had an extremely negative outlook on life, and I began to spend the majority of my time outside of work around this person. I am an eternal optimist, but I found myself starting to become more negative. This person blamed the world for his problems, and at first, I thought I could help him take accountability for his life and stop self-destructing. My dear friends reading this book, never enter into a relationship with anyone who is on a completely different path. This individual was toxic to himself and everyone around him. He refused to acknowledge his own tendencies to self-destruct, and I ultimately had to remove myself from this destruction.

This was my first big lesson in realizing that taking accountability is a personal choice and cannot be forced on someone who is unwilling to be open to change or self-improvement. I think there are many of us who want to "help" people see their true potential, but we need to be careful not to allow these people into our inner circle unless they are actively seeking change. I cannot have a positive effect on anyone's life who isn't open to change or doesn't desire change. Each of us is on a path. Some people seek enlightenment, others seek success, and some embrace it all. Surround yourself with people who want to evolve and are constantly seeking growth. Do not waste your time with those that don't.

The people with whom we surround ourselves are the biggest influence on our own behavior, attitude, and results. Ask yourself this very important question: do the people in my circle motivate me or drain me? Your inner circle of friends has probably changed since high school. I am not saying that those friendships should be ignored or dissolved because of differences in lifestyle or goals, but we do have to be careful where and with whom we spend our time. If a friendship is true, nothing can dissolve it. Who you choose to spend time with is your choice. If you choose to surround yourself with people who are uninspired or unhappy, you will soon find your life yielding the same results.

When it comes to your circle of friends, the bigger the better, right? Not necessarily. You need to carefully select who is in your most-trusted inner circle, and you'll be surprised at how much of a difference that alone will make in your life. Because the prevailing assumption when it comes to, well, just about anything, is: the more, the better, it's only natural for us to want to supersize our network of connections—both online and off. After all, the more people we know, the greater our chances of being exposed to opportunities that may lead to professional advancement, potential mentors, material success, and so on, right? In fact, it is more important to surround ourselves with a carefully curated group of people whom we admire and respect and with whom we share common beliefs and values—people who will set the tone for the foundation of our larger network filled with people who provide value to one another. And that core group should be a lot smaller than you likely think.

We're all time-deprived; it can be daunting to have to manage work, family, and the "spare" time we spend on the necessary evil we call networking. But networking doesn't have to be so time-consuming. If you're like most people, you have built your network haphazardly, connecting with anyone who will communicate with you. You probably have a hard time saying no to people. And, as a result, people you barely know are probably making demands on your time and, like a true good Samaritan, you may be accommodating them. But your undiscerning generosity may be self-defeating; by giving your time to fifty people rather than, say, five, you are making far less of an impact in the world than the sheer volume of your network would have you think.

It is important to consider the people who are in your inner circle because they are going to deeply and profoundly influence you. People are going to make snap judgements of you based on your inner circle. That doesn't mean that you should try to populate your inner circle with high-profile contacts whose shine will rub off on you; it means that it's important to seek out and nurture relationships with good, smart people who have your best interests at heart. You need to be ruthlessly selective, because everyone in your core group also has an inner circle with which you will ultimately be connected, and those people will have an inner circle, and so on.

So, how do you go about building your own strong inner circle?

First, assess yourself. Are you in control of the relationships in your life, or are you giving that control to others? That standing lunch date, or the conference you've attended for years because your friend is involved—when was the last time those interactions provided value to you or allowed you to provide value to someone else? Do you come away energized or drained? If you are not deciding upon the rules of engagement and making deliberate choices about who you are spending time with, you need to take back that control. Start by making a plan to lessen your time investment in people and activities that make unrewarding demands on you until you can fully withdraw from the person, commitment, or activity.

Second, assess your habits and activities. What activities did you take part in over the past week? What was worth your time? What wasn't? What would you definitely do again or invest more time in? What would you cut entirely? Also ask yourself if the way you're spending your time is aligned with your most deeply-held values. If it's not, drop the activity, even if it has the potential to put you in an uncomfortable position with friends or colleagues.

Finally, assess others. Who did you recently spend time with? What types of people do you want to spend more time with, and what types do you want to cut out completely? Remember that relationships should not be transactional—the idea is not to spend time only with people who you believe can help you. Rather, consider the long-term value of building mutually-beneficial relationships. Super-connectors are always on the lookout for ways to help others, not because there is the expectation of reciprocity but because being useful and generous builds social capital by making you valuable and memorable.

As you shrink your inner circle, you'll begin thinking of yourself as the architect of your environment. As you forge deeper, more authentic relationships with smaller numbers of people who are genuinely important to you, you will gain more context into their wants and needs, and they will likewise develop a fuller understanding of you.

Do you want to be successful? You will never achieve success if your inner circle is full of unsuccessful people. If you have someone in your life who is constantly negative, but you feel that it is your responsibility to "save" them or "change" them, you need to find a way to limit or outright exclude them from your life.

Do you want to be happy? Surround yourself with people who choose to be happy.

Do you want to be a millionaire? The best place to start is by looking for mentors who are, themselves, millionaires.

During my own accountability assessment, I took a hard look at my inner circle, wrote down everyone I was spending time with, and assigned them a number between one and ten. I made a decision when I was finished to keep only the "tens" because I did not want an average life. I had put in the work and stopped being a people-pleaser. I had changed the way I said things and was beginning to realize the power of affirmations and manifestation. I was being responsible and accountable to myself. I was feeling better than I had in years. But I noticed that all these exciting things that were happening in my life were being judged by some of my friends. It was as though I woke up one day and didn't have anything to talk about with certain friends I had known for years. I still valued their friendship, but I wasn't getting anything out of it. We had grown apart and no longer had nothing in common.

I found myself engaging in amazing conversations with strangers at the bookstore but having boring conversations with my friends over the phone. I had to take action, because I knew there was more available to me. So, I went back to my number system to assess the rank of my current inner circle. The "tens" were the people I was excited to talk to, learned from, and loved being around. They provided value by sharing knowledge and pushing me to set more goals.

Once I had completed the audit, I was certain that I would miss those people that I could no longer spend time with, but as the months passed, I noticed that we had stayed in touch. We remained friends. They simply were no longer in the inner circle.

Out of all of my friends at the time, I rated thirty-three. Can you guess how many I put into my inner circle?

One.

I had one person who I could rank as a ten on the "friendship mutual value" scale, so that person is the only person who remained in my inner circle and she's still there to this day. Everyone else I've added to my inner circle is a "ten." They represent both who I am and who I want to be. The common denominator we all share is a thirst for knowledge, a drive for success, and a commitment to make each other better. They are my greatest teachers, biggest cheerleaders, and most trusted confidants.

Let's now move out of our inner circle and talk about our friends in general. The people just outside the inner circle who might move in one day or sift through for a season.

Everyone needs friends. We are social creatures who thrive off of connections with others. We need friends to hold a mirror up to us and show us what our behavior looks like. They provide companionship and support, but the most important thing friends do is help us work out who we are. Family members cannot do that in quite the same way.

It's important to be strategic in our friendships. People think friends just magically appear out of nowhere, and they complain when they don't have any. You need to strongly consider, What do I need from my friends, and am I being a good friend in return?

With that in mind, how many friends can one person reasonably give quality support? Psychologists use the term "affiliation need," and society tells us that we have a lot of it. Affiliation need is defined as a person's need to feel a sense of involvement and "belonging" within a social group. This "need" is driven by one of human beings' most basic and universal motivations: the desire to interact and take pleasure in being with others. In truth, some people need a lot of friends; others only need a few. There are specific types of friendships you should look to form throughout your lifetime. A good solid circle of friends should contain some of these qualities below. Some people in your circle might be several of the examples below but if your circle contains three people or thirty-three people keep your inner circle tight. Your circle may contain thirty-three people but that inner circle should be the people you speak to frequently and spend the most time with. Who in your circle have the following qualities?

Motivators/Inspirational Leaders

These are the friends who motivate you, help you see your strengths, advise you on how best to use those strengths, and are generous with their time.

Loyalty Leaders (Ride or Die)

These are the friends who stand up for you and your beliefs and praise you to everyone they know.

Connectors

These are the friends who get to know you and then instantly work to connect you with their contacts who share your interests or goals.

Collaborators

Collaborators are friends with similar interests; they are the people with whom you are most likely to spend your time.

High Energy Captains

These friends are fun and cheer you up when you're down. They always make themselves available to boost your spirits.

Creatives

Creatives stretch your viewpoint, and introduce you to new ideas, opportunities, and culture.

Navigators

These are friends you seek out when you need guidance and counsel; they're great at talking through your options.

Companions

Companions are the first people you call, with either good news or bad. They are always there for you.

Now that you know what type of friends you will benefit from having in your world, start looking for meaningful relationships and connect with the right people so that you can contribute to enhancing other people's lives and they can start enhancing yours. Life is far too short to feel obligated to be friends with someone or to engage in a friendship that is one-sided or not positive. Wish those people the best, and find different friends. Those people are no longer your people!

Eliminating people from your inner circle is definitely not easy. The process requires you to be honest with yourself and reflect on who in your life is pushing you toward greatness as well as celebrating your successes. Pay close attention to those who clap only for themselves; they do not belong in your inner circle.

Our inner circles may change over time, or they may stay relatively the same, but you need to perform audits at different points in your life to most effectively get you where you are going. Surround yourself with what you want your life to mirror, and before you know it, that will be your life. The people you have around you will have a direct impact on your success and happiness.

ACCOUNTABILITY STEP

List the five people you spend the most time with every week. Do they fit into one of the above categories? Or, do you need to conduct an inner-circle audit party?

CHAPTER EIGHT

SWIM WITH SHARKS WHO HAVE PURPOSE

We just talked about how important your inner circle is, but what about the environment in which you place yourself?

As I mentioned before, I've spent my entire career in the automotive industry, an industry that has taught me so much about the business world. For those of you who are not familiar with the women-to-men ratio in my field, I was very much considered a minority as a woman. There are wonderful conferences now for women in this industry to come together and learn from each other, but when I was new to the industry those awesome support systems were not available. In the beginning of my career, it was tough. For the most part, the only females were receptionists or office staff. So many people asked me why I chose to work in that cut-throat environment, and the answer at the time was simple: money.

I was twenty years old, and I was the only female sales consultant on staff. I knew nothing about cars, but I was confident that I could talk to people. I had zero training, and I had a manager who threw around the term "sink or swim" like confetti. I loved helping people and finding out about their lives, and I very quickly started outselling the men on staff. I was going to college and working at the same time, making more money than I'd ever made in my life. I had a boyfriend who worked at a gym as a private trainer, and I was earning triple his income. I felt on top of the world—until I continued to sell more and more cars.

The men I worked with were supportive and helpful at first, but as my success grew, their friendships started to retreat. This was the beginning of my growth in terms of not letting someone else's words or opinion ruin my day. I'd dismiss or completely ignore the negative comments, but as a young woman, they hurt my feelings. They were all so nice to my face, so I was shocked that they would say things behind my back that were so untrue. I was, by far, the youngest and I watched these men make up lies about me when I outsold them.

This was a pivotal learning lesson for me in business: haters are going to hate. I decided after a year that I wanted to get off the sales floor and learn finance. I went to my general manager and told him what I wanted to do, but he said no. I immediately got a box and started to pack up my things, and he ran over and asked me if I was going to quit if I didn't get a chance in the Finance and Insurance department. I looked up, said yes, and he started to laugh. He told me I could start learning the following day.

I spent the next twelve months working fourteen hours a day, six days a week, to learn Finance and Insurance. I got to attend a finance school, but I had to pick up the Finance and Insurance Director's dry cleaning and bring him coffee in exchange. The training was brutal, but I did it, and I became very good at it.

I replaced the director in a short amount of time and was running the department. I loved training the producers (my staff), and I never asked anyone to pick up my dry cleaning or my coffee! I loved having a team, and for the next twelve years, I worked in Finance and Insurance departments for different dealer groups representing multiple manufacturers. I realized that I needed to move into different positions to achieve a greater understanding of other departments and asked for the opportunity to manage the sales team as well as work in various management roles to gain a good understanding of each department.

My daughter was born in 2012, and afterward, I was given the opportunity to take a platform executive corporate director role and manage the F&I departments for a thirty-store group. This opportunity allowed me to spend weekends with my child and experience a good work/life balance. While this is not the end of my career story, I'm going to take a break here to talk about the importance of our work environments.

I have so much empathy for people who say that they hate their job. The reality is that some of those people do not actually hate the actual task or "job" they are doing, they are merely in an unhealthy environment that doesn't make them feel valuable. If you ask someone who "hates" their job why they feel that way, they'll often respond with an excuse centered around how they feel at their job, which often includes one or more of the following: unappreciated, under-utilized, demoralized, not connected, and/or not challenged. Put simply, if you—as a leader—are not connecting and communicating clearly with your staff, you will end up with employees who "hate" their job.

It took me a long time to recognize the difference between an unhealthy and a healthy work environment. I have had both the pleasure and the unpleasant experience of working in both. Culture within the environment of a workspace determines the tone and productivity of the staff. The workplace culture that an employer supports and teaches (or tolerates and ignores) will determine the cycle of turnover with their staff.

Culture is driven by behavior.

Work culture is interpreted differently by different employees. Events in people's lives affect the way they act and interact at work. Even when an organization has a common culture, each person may see that culture from a different perspective.

While not synonymous, employee engagement and culture are certainly linked together. Since engagement is largely about how employees feel as they approach their work, a positive culture is fundamental to building an engaged team.

Leaders also mistakenly assume that culture is a purely internal phenomenon. The thing is, external results are driven by internal cultural norms and behaviors. Therefore, since your company's internal culture affects the way the people in your organization work, that culture also inevitably influences your company's product, including your brand and customer service.

The essence of culture and the reason it's so important is that it's a set of norms that help inform both the way you make decisions and the way you treat people, both of which touch every aspect of your business. The heart of your business actually is your culture, and it will have a direct impact on your success.

To mitigate the natural tendency of employees to use only the components of the culture that serve their needs, you must teach and model the culture you desire. Frequent reinforcement of the desired culture demonstrates the aspects of your work environment you most want to see repeated and rewarded. If you practice this reinforcement regularly, employees can more easily support the culture you wish to reinforce.

Positive attitudes and positive actions make for a positive workplace culture. Foster collaboration and communication, and encourage leadership and management styles that strengthen teamwork. Open and honest communication is vital to creating a positive feeling in the workplace. Open and honest communication also requires that regular audits are taken to evaluate the ways people are interacting with each other. Feedback is welcomed, and opportunities for social interaction are enabled. These can include coffee mornings, team getaways, and family weekends and gives an opportunity for team members to nurture and foster connections outside of work. Continued learning opportunities that enable team members to assess their inherent unconscious and implicit biases, biases that can impact their interactions with other employees, are crucial. Also, strict no-tolerance open-door policies and complaint procedures for workplace bullying are crucial for creating a positive collaborative environment.

It's also important to create an inclusive work environment where all employees feel valued, supported, and nurtured, irrespective of gender, sexual orientation, or race. All employees should have equal opportunities to progress and equal access to all the perks and rewards available. An inclusive workplace is one that values individual differences and makes everyone feel welcome and accepted. Include signage that supports inclusivity and ensure that it's clear and positive. Language choices can create issues related to confusion and miscommunication. Careful use of language that reinforces a gender-conscious and inclusive ethos is important.

Your work culture may be strong, or it may be weak. When it's strong, most people in the group agree on it. When it's weak, people do not agree on it. Sometimes a weak organizational culture is the result of many subcultures or the shared values, assumptions, and behaviors of a subset of the organization.

For example, the culture of your company as a whole might be weak and difficult to characterize because there are so many subcultures within it. Each department or team may have its own culture. Within departments, the staff and managers may each have their own culture.

A good, productive, company-wide culture supports a positive and productive environment.

Happy employees are not necessarily productive employees nor are productive employees necessarily happy employees. It is important to find aspects of the culture that will support each of these qualities to retain employees and give them a reason to "love" their career.

I wasted so much energy when I was younger trying to create an atmosphere of change and positivity for automotive dealers who were not in tune with the power of positivity. I was also fortunate enough to work with some employers along my career path who did have a culture of positivity and happy employees. Those employers were few and far between fifteen or twenty years ago, but I now see more and more automotive industry leaders stepping up the way I did, trying to change the environment for both the customer and employee experience.

I became determined to invest in myself in order to become a stronger leader. I worked with many managers throughout my career but only a few phenomenal leaders. I noticed very quickly that the stores that had good leadership and trained their managers to lead instead of simply to manage had massive success. The staff was happy, and the energy on the showroom floor was positive and contagious. People wanted to be at work, and there was always excitement in the air. Negative employees didn't have to be fired they quit on their own when they figured out that they didn't belong.

Starting to see the positive shift that the auto industry is taking is exciting, and it reconfirms what I already knew: the energy passed down from the leadership to the staff will determine the culture and future success of a store.

The point of this chapter is that, to be successful, you have to live in your purpose. If you have to swim with the sharks, make sure they are the sharks who have purpose. When you're "walking in purpose"—that is, engaged with and working toward your purpose life becomes easier, less complicated, and less stressful. You become more focused, like an arrow flying toward its target, and your mind feels strong, with less space available for negativity to seep in.

Time is precious, and if you are swimming with sharks in muddy waters (in other words, sharks that have little-to-no purpose), you will never be able to see where you are going. The environment that you work in will have a huge impact on your career path. Do you want a clear path with leaders who can help you grow and learn? Or, do you want to aimlessly swim around, hoping that you are going the right direction? Swim with sharks that have purpose. Don't waste your time with those just looking for food.

I now only have the desire to be in productive environments with winners and industry leaders. I am asking you to have the same standards for yourself. In what kind of environment do you work now? Do you have a clearly defined career path with leaders who are supportive and collaborative? Do you work among managers who send out to-do lists but never motivate or inspire? Does your employer make you feel valuable and worthy?

All of these questions are intended to get you thinking about your life. You should love your career. If you don't, make a change. If you are in an unhealthy environment, find a different job. Stop settling.

If you are considering settling for an average life, go back and reread this book from the beginning. Ask yourself the question "whose life will be negatively impacted if I only strive for average" The most important person that choice affects is YOU. Don't settle for average. You are designed for greatness. You have a gift, and it is up to you to identify it. You can monetize your gift and follow your passion to live your best life. If what you are doing to generate income feels like "work," you are cheating yourself out of the happiness that comes from living a purpose-driven life. The choice is yours to make.

ACCOUNTABILITY STEP

If you find that you have a job or career rather than a true calling, spend some time journaling about your goals. Can you incorporate your calling into your current career? What do you really want to be doing in a decade?

CHAPTER NINE

ALL THAT GLITTERS IS NOT GOLD

I loved my job and all of the F&I managers I was responsible for, but I was ready to take my career to the next level. I started as a sales consultant, moved into the role of F&I manager, F&I director, Sales Manager, and back to a F&I Director. I got married and later got pregnant with my daughter. I had tried for so long to become pregnant, and after several miscarriages, I was finally able to carry to term. I was so excited that I was finally going to have a baby, and as soon as I found out that I was having a girl, I was overwhelmed with gratitude and pure joy. I left the auto industry and stayed at home with her for about a year and a half, and when I was ready to go back to work, I took the platform position as an executive director of finance and development for a group with thirty stores. This position was demanding, but I loved it. I loved training the F&I departments and spending time in the stores. It was great for a few years, but my own past inability to say no started creeping up on me.

Once again, I began taking on additional responsibilities and saying yes to every request my boss put in front of me. I found myself on a rigorous travel schedule (with a three-year-old at home), trying to balance my daughter and a pending divorce. I was feeling stressed and not centered; I was walking a tightrope. I quickly became keenly aware that my work/life balance was non-existent and it would only be a matter of time before all the extra responsibilities coupled with travel was going to put my health at risk. I began to start setting boundaries and eliminating activity traps in my life. That was when I was given an opportunity to reach one of my long-term goals. I was asked if I wanted to take a risk and become a General Manager.

I accepted the offer to become the GM of an automotive dealership. This dealership was in another state, so it required that I take a risk by moving and taking on a struggling store. This was my first time in the general manager role, but I was ready and excited to bring change and lasting results to this store. I had dreams of growing the store and expanding, and I wanted to eventually buy into my own store. I had processes and procedures I was going to implement to change the way consumers purchased cars. I was determined to lead the charge when it came to erasing the negative stigma associated with the industry. I wanted to empower female consumers as well as inspire women to choose a career in automotive. I was on fire and beyond excited to take on the looming responsibility. I planned to triple the volume and quadruple the net profit. I was excited to inspire other women to advocate for themselves and seek out the opportunities that they deserve.

Fast-forward to my first day running the dealership.

The dealership was in a beautiful area, but the store itself was outdated and in desperate need of some attention. I will never forget the way it felt walking in to meet my staff. That day is such a fond memory for me, and it still makes me smile when I think about it. That is, until I remember the customer who walked onto the showroom floor demanding to speak to the general manager. I immediately slipped into my role and introduced myself to the client who, in turn, asked me where my dad was.

For those of you who aren't in the automotive industry, it was at that time extraordinarily rare for a woman to be a general manager, and this man absolutely could not imagine that I occupied that role unless my dad owned the store. Let that sink in for a moment. This was right before the #metoo movement was in full swing and focus was directed at shattering glass ceilings. I had spent the previous seventeen years of my life in the automotive industry, working in various management positions with male-dominated staff, dreaming of the day when I'd get my opportunity to become a GM. I politely introduced myself (again) and asked if he would like to follow me to my office so we could discuss his grievances in private. He looked me up and down and told me that while I was a "good-looking gal," he would just come back when my dad was there. I tried a third time to tell him that no one in my family was or had ever been in the automotive industry, but I was happy to help him with whatever he needed help with. He turned and walked out of the store, and I never saw him again. This started the uphill battle that I would navigate for the duration of my time at the store.

I started to settle in to my new role and was interviewed by a local magazine running a story about the fact that I was the only female general manager in the area. I had so much fun recording our radio ads and even had my daughter appear on a few. I showed my staff that I was willing to "walk the walk." I took a hands-on approach, and because of my background, I was happy to be involved working deals in the tower, spinning deals in finance, and closing deals on the floor. I was a servant leader who had empathy for my staff. I implemented processes and best practices that I had collected over my many years in the industry.

I worked hard to create the type of culture I had always wanted to work in. I took my experiences from the best automotive dealerships I had worked for and combined the positive things about their cultures into what I thought was the perfect environment. I wanted to empower my staff to become the best that they could be. Think Tony Robbins meets corporate America. I looked at this opportunity as my shot to prove not only to myself but to every man in this industry that women make great GMs in automotive. I wanted to prove that we are just as capable as men and can not only take a struggling store and turn it around but also make a huge impact on the industry itself.

I am confident that I did the best I could with what I was given. It was a small store filled with challenges, obstacles, and more than a few employees who did not want to take direction from a woman. I had so many plans for that store, but the reality was that I was not a partner in the store, just a GM. I had to get all operational changes approved by the store partners before I could implement real change, and most of the time, my recommendations were dismissed or outright denied. I was a process-driven person who had to learn how to be adaptable in an environment where I did not have the support to truly make major changes. The time I spent out of state while running that store was an awesome education. I loved being a GM, and I will forever be grateful to the people who gave me the opportunity.

Once I got the store profitable, the dealer principals who owned it made the decision to sell the dealership, and I parted ways with my employer. I put the house I had purchased on the market and packed up myself and my daughter to head back home to Texas to start the next phase of my career. I felt like a failure at the time even though the store had become more profitable. Even though I had increased profitability, I couldn't revolutionize the store and wipe out all the negative stigmas surrounding the industry I loved. In the entire scope of my career, this was the experience that had provided me with the most growth. I was aware before I took the opportunity that they were actively trying to sell the store, but I chose to look at the opportunity through rose-colored glasses and just jump in.

I had successes and failures, but most of all, I gained knowledge and experience. People ask me all the time if I would do it all over again, and the answer will always be absolutely yes. I would not be who I am today if I had never taken that risk and jumped into that opportunity. I met some of the nicest, most genuine people during my time there, and they will always hold a special place in my heart.

Do not be afraid to take risks. Things will not always work out as you plan, and what appears at first to glitter may not end up being gold, but you will get out of it what you need to at the time. If your self-worth revolves around your title or your paycheck, you're headed for disappointment. If we confuse our identity with our earning potential, we will sacrifice our relationships and our health to gain more money. That includes our mental health. I urge you to rethink how you define success.

ACCOUNTABILITY STEP

A difficult step for leaders is learning to let go and trust your team to carry the load farther than you can on your own. List the strengths and weaknesses of each person on your team, and purposefully reflect on how you can enhance their strengths and strengthen their weaknesses.

CHAPTER TEN

TRUST YOUR INTUITION

S top second-guessing yourself. The first instinct you have is always right if you have opened yourself up and learned to listen to your built-in safety net. Your intuition gives you clues about other people by assessing the energy that they push out into the world. I have opened myself up to the point where I can read someone just by the energy they are putting into the world. I was in a situation not too long ago where I wanted to meet a particular person who I heard about through friends but had never been around in person. I got within three feet of him and realized that I didn't even want to shake his hand. His energy was so bad that I wasn't even willing to stand next to him.

I have also experienced the opposite effect and met a man who had amazing, inviting energy that was happy and authentic. You have to stop doubting your instincts and trust that first reaction. Your mind has the ability to calculate risk and allow your body to feel energy on a spiritual level. I have legitimately been in places where I have thought to myself, "Why am I even here? This situation brings zero value into my life." 100 percent of the time, my natural intuition about the situation was correct.

Let's return to our discussion about people. There are three things to look for when you are engaging with people but are not face-to-face. With social media and technology platforms becoming so advanced, we connect with people superficially, and that can be a disadvantage. There is no energy in a text, so you have to learn to listen to your intuition. The three types of people to avoid connecting with on any social platform are silent haters, instigators, and predatory people. Before I go deeper into this, I want to make it clear that your friend list on social media is going to contain some of these people. I don't recommend that you delete them, but "love them from afar" if you see any clues that they fit into any of these categories. The only way you can achieve your destiny is by having the clarity that comes from an environment that can sustain your success. I have had to make painful decisions and remove people from my life who I loved but who were toxic to my existence.

Silent haters fly under the radar. We all know what a hater is, and these people make it obvious as they troll the internet looking for someone to discredit or insult in order to make themselves feel more valuable. Silent haters are a different breed altogether, but they are easy to pick out.

Imagine the core network of followers that you engage with. You likely have people who show support but don't actively engage. Those connections are valuable. Silent haters, on the other hand, will engage with you only if they are looking to capitalize on a situation. They will act like a chameleon in different groups in an attempt to gain followers at any cost. They will look to discredit others and will never show support. These people are not your people, and even if you show support for them, they won't reciprocate. Leave them in your friend list or Instagram feed if you choose, but refrain from connecting on a deeper level.

Instigators are always looking to spark an unhealthy conversation or debate. Conversation should be non-combative and genuine. The person asking for an opinion or advice doesn't really want it if what they are clearly looking for is little more than a fight. Again, do not engage. Keep scrolling, and don't spend any energy getting into a verbal game of chess. Rise above anything petty and narrow-minded, and keep in mind that most of the time these instigators have a purpose for everything they post. Once again, do not engage.

Predatory people are everywhere, and your natural intuition will protect you from these people if you learn to trust it! Predatory people are those who will befriend you and infiltrate themselves into your life purely for financial gain. They are manipulators who will speak unkindly of others to execute their own agendas. This type of person truly represents the way the scientific aspect of intuition comes into play and can help prevent them from ever getting close to you. I am going to provide you with the definition of intuition, and I want you to fully absorb the meaning of the word.

Intuition (noun): The ability to understand something immediately without the need for conscious reasoning. This word is of Latin origin and is defined as denoting spiritual insight or immediate spiritual communication.

Maya Angelou summed it up best:

"You are the sum total of everything that you've ever seen, heard, eaten, smelled, been told, forgot it's all there. Everything influences each of us, and because of that I try to make sure that my experiences are positive."

Intuition is actually our brain drawing on past experiences and cumulative knowledge. It is our brain on autopilot, performing the action of processing information without our conscious mind even being aware of it. The automatic information processing happens all day, every day. One example of this process is something every one of us has experienced.

We've all experienced getting in a car and starting to drive to a destination but getting distracted thinking about other things while on the way. You may drive for an hour lost in thought, only to suddenly "end up" in your driveway. You don't remember stopping at red lights or passing cars; you drove the entire distance unaware that we were driving. You drove for miles without a conscious thought about the activity of driving the car, but you did it and got there safe. That is an example of the way intuition works for everyone. Our minds have the natural ability to alert us to danger. We only need to trust what our mind is telling us.

Predatory people who will try to wedge their way into your life are focused on preying on you to satisfy their agenda. They will use every tool in their toolbox to make you feel obligated to do whatever it is that they want you to do. These people will try to convince you that they are genuine. They will use trickery and stroke your ego by showering you with compliments to drive a certain result. They will confide in you and trust you with information about other people to make you feel special or important. Trust your intuition. Go with your gut. These people thrive on the big close and spend their entire life looking for victims. These are not your people. They are chameleons who say and do whatever they need to in order to get what they want.

Harnessing the power of intuition in your own life will help you make better decisions and protect you from predatory people. Intuition is not, however, a replacement for logic. Learning to use both in every decision in your life will help you get to the next level. Our minds are so powerful, yet only a small fraction of people ever truly harness the power that we have. Regardless of your religious beliefs or spiritual affiliations, there is no denying that we have so many gifts at our disposal, and our bodies are magnificent. It is amazing what we are capable of and the greatness that we all possess.

ACCOUNTABILITY STEP

The next time you have a big idea, explore it as far as it will go. Don't let anyone talk you out of it until you have done all the research and planning. Use your intuition as a guide and brainstorm creative ways to make your big idea become a reality.

CHAPTER ELEVEN

CONSISTENTLY MANIFEST POSITIVE RESULTS

At this point in my career, I'm at a place where I consistently trust my instincts and I use information and data to drive results. I also use another technique that I want to share with you. I was a huge skeptic when I started using it, but I gave it a shot anyway after becoming aware of how powerful our minds are and how much control we have over our flow of energy. We have been given a powerful gift that we can utilize to achieve success. I could write an entire (separate) book on manifestation techniques, but I want to briefly give you some tips that you can apply now to take control of your destiny.

Let It Go

The first part of successful manifestation is letting go. Before you can manifest anything, you have to let go of those things that will interrupt your thought cycle. Negative thoughts are a good example of a barrier that will prevent manifestation from working. You need to center yourself and get into a state of meditation to truly be effective. Meditation is an excellent way to get into the state in which you'll know exactly what to ask for from the universe. You have to be clear on what you want in order to take steps to make it happen. If you are not extremely specific about what you want, you will not be able to direct energy toward it. An example of the way a broad manifestation could yield undesirable results is the following statement: "I want a vacation" (It's unspecific and open to interpretation). You then receive a call from your company, letting you know that they are downsizing, and you are going to be let go. Welcome to the universe's interpretation of a vacation!

Another example: "I want a fourteen-day trip to Hawaii to experience the beauty of the world." This declaration is specific. Manifestations are strong, so you must be very clear and specific about what you want.

Once you know exactly what you want, it is time to ask the universe for it. Think of manifestation as co-creation between you and the universe. There are lots of ways to ask the universe for what you want. You can pray for it, meditate on it, visualize it, use a vision board, or employ a combination of all of them. I use a combination, but the best approach is specific to each individual, and it needs to include whatever avenues you connect with best.

Create a Vision Board

Vision boards are one of my favorite ways to begin manifesting my desires. They are a great reminder and motivator to keep our goals in the forefront of our minds. A vision board can be anything that you can keep in your line of sight. My vision board hangs in my office and contains pictures and phrases that I am currently manifesting. You need to update your vision board regularly and look at it as frequently as possible.

If you are manifesting a trip to Hawaii, for example, cut out pictures off Hawaii and put them all over your board. Spend time in meditation thinking about the sand in Hawaii, feeling the breeze coming off the ocean, and smelling the tropical flowers. Focus on the calmness of your body lying on the beach, looking at the ocean. Picture in your mind's eye the photos of Hawaii that you have put on your vision board. Picture them in detail. Go over every detail in your mind, and then start speaking your affirmations.

Specific, targeted affirmations in this example could include:

"I am going to Hawaii."

"I am going to feel the breeze and walk on the sand in Hawaii."

"I am attracting positive energy and opportunities that will allow me to go to Hawaii."

Never use negative words; remember, you are making this happen with the help of the universe.

Take Action

The next part of making manifestation work for you is taking action. You have to help the universe; you're co-creating with it! So, you need to do things to direct the flow of energy in the proper direction. When you start to see the act of manifesting working, acknowledge what is being sent to you.

You must increase your flow of energy or heighten your vibration. According to the Law of Attraction, you will attract that which you are sending out.

Everything in our world is energy. Our thoughts are energy, and the things we want to bring into our lives are also energy. When two energies are similar, they come together like a moth to a flame. Because we can control our thoughts, we can control what happens in our lives to a large degree. Focusing on positive experiences brings positive experiences; focusing on negative brings negative.

"You will notice that those who speak of most prosperity, have it. Those who speak most of health, have

it. Those who speak most of poverty, have it. It is
Law. It can be no other way... The way you feel is
your point of attraction, and so, the Law of Attraction
is most understood when you see yourself as a magnet
getting more and more of the way you feel. When you
feel lonely, you attract more loneliness. When you
feel poor, you attract more poverty. When you feel
sick, you attract more sickness. When you feel unhappy, you attract more unhappiness. When you feel
healthy and vital and alive and prosperous, you attract
more of all of those things."
—*The Teachings of Abraham*

To attract more of what you want, you need to
raise your vibration. If you want to attract success,
start planning for your definition of success. Educate
and invest in yourself to develop actionable goals,
direct as much energy as you can toward it, and you
will see it manifest.

ACCOUNTABILITY STEP

Start a vision board. Go out and purchase a cork
board that you can hang in an area of your home or
office where you're forced to look at it several times a
day (don't forget the push pins!). Cut out pictures or

words that represent your goals as visual reminders and post them on the board.

CHAPTER TWELVE

LEAVE YOUR EGO AT THE DOOR

The Freudian concept of ego is that it represents one of three constructs in Sigmund Freud's structural model of the psyche. Socially, we have words derived from ego, including egoism, egotism, and egocentrism. As a woman who has worked in a highly competitive, male-dominated industry, I understand all three very well.

Egoism is an ethical theory that treats self-interest as the foundation of morality.

Egotism is the drive to maintain and enhance favorable views of oneself.

Egocentrism is the inability to differentiate between self and other.

The three E's are valuable to recognize in yourself and others. You have to first understand what each one is to be able to identify them and take appropriate action, however. Remember earlier when we discussed predatory people? All predatory people are at least one of these three E's.

Ego, in and of itself, is not negative. We should have a high opinion of ourselves and know our worth, but that doesn't mean that we shouldn't also be humble and grateful. Being a confident person who is secure in his or her abilities is wonderful, but falling into one of the three E's can get a person into a situation where their once positive energy turns negative and invites negativity into their life. Let's talk about ego in business.

We have likely all heard the phrase "Leaders lead, and managers manage." I believe this wholeheartedly, but have you ever really thought about what the great differentiator between leaders and managers? It's ego. Ego is one of the biggest problems that employers face when trying to identify good leaders over basic managers when hiring.

A strong ego will cause a manager to be afraid to push and try new things in order to grow. Ego will make him or her complacent and stagnant in their thinking. If you are a team member looking for opportunities to advance, the best thing you can do is, check your ego. Do you demonstrate the characteristics of a servant leader, or is every decision you make self-centered? Standing out from the crowd and not allowing yourself to be directed by ego is not easy, but it's definitely worth it if you are looking to advance in your company. Leaders are humble. They have a sincere servant attitude and are laser focused on driving results. Humility is the single most important attribute in identifying true leaders who will motivate your staff and take your company to the next level.

The ego-less leader recognizes her own strengths and can identify the gaps in her skill set. She will make hiring decisions to fill in those gaps to build the right team for her organization. Those managers who operate with too-strong egos open themselves up to manipulation. People who are ego driven are predictable and self-serving. Unhealthily strong egos crave massive amounts of positive attention, which will distract them from their responsibilities. When you are a victim of your own need to be seen as great, you open yourself up not only to manipulation but to bad decisions that can affect the people for whom you are responsible.

Emotional Intelligence is a highly underrated quality. Employers aim to find high achievers who are driven and confident, but they drastically underestimate the power of emotional intelligence when leading a team or running a business. As a leader, your job is to use diligent, mindful effort to stay grounded and in touch with the way the decisions you make affect the people for whom you are responsible. If you hire a manager who cannot manage his own emotions or the emotions of his staff, you are not hiring someone who is capable enough to lead. The ability to motivate, cheer up, or calm down other people is a superpower that emotionally intelligent people are able to harness.

A good leader is not afraid to hire someone who has a bigger skill set or is "better than them," at least in some areas. They are ambitious for the company, not just themselves, and they possess a strong sense of humility. They use emotional intelligence to connect with and have synergy with their staff and drive the results they want while motivating and inspiring.

Let's all commit to hiring good leaders and developing good leadership skills at every level of an organization. If we all become strong leaders, we will see employee satisfaction go up and companies' profits soar. Stop feeding (or being) an ego monster and perpetuating negative stigmas. Become a leader in your own right, in any situation.

ACCOUNTABILITY STEP

At your next big meeting, make sure to create time for everyone to speak, regardless of their role or tenure with the company. A good leader makes every employee feel valued and worthy of contributing valuable opinions and ideas.

CHAPTER THIRTEEN

FOCUS ON SIMPLIFICATION

S ometimes, as high achievers, we overthink situations and live in a constant state of excess. I have always had lots of things. I found myself going into my closet and standing there, thinking to myself, "I have nothing to wear" when, in fact, I barely had any room left on the racks. I have valued a huge walk-in closet in every home I've lived in. I came to a standoff with my closet when I got to the point where I was literally spending more time standing in it, staring at all the excess and choices, then actually getting ready. I started noticing that it was taking longer and longer for me to make a decision about what I was going to wear for meetings, to the office, and even to take my daughter to dance class. My college days spent throwing on yoga pants and an inspirational T-shirt seemed to have gotten lost in the transition to the business world. I have always enjoyed dressing up and have a vast wardrobe of business clothes, but as I have gotten older, the ability to just throw on something has become a struggle.

I started to look at the root of this uncharacteristic indecisiveness in order to dissect how I could fix it. I began to recognize that I would change into and out of clothes several times (while still in my closet) and get frustrated when something didn't fit the way I remembered. I'd put the item that I was frustrated with back in its place, and several months later, grab it again only to re-experience the same scenario. On so many levels, this was such a waste of time. If I truly wanted to maximize my time and increase the level of productivity and positivity in my life, things had to change.

It sounds incredibly simple to say, "Just be organized." I would actually credit my organizational skills as one of the elements that has allowed me to achieve success in my life. Having been that way for as long as I can remember, I had to wonder why those skills hadn't made their way into my closet?!

Granted, I had everything organized, shoes by heel height, pants with pants (dark colors to light), dresses by length and occasion, and everything by color and item type. Friends who walked into my closet understandably assumed that I was organized to the degree that there was no way I could be having such a hard time with the simple task of trying to get ready for work every morning. However, the disruption that my closet was creating in my life was becoming laughable, and it was not utilizing my time-management skills. I knew I couldn't be the only person who started off her day by getting up early, creating a gratitude list, having a few cups of coffee before my daughter needed to get up for school, taking a shower, having an amazing hair day, and then *BAM!* I'd hit a brick wall when it came to what I wanted to wear.

I have always loved silk, kimono-style robes, and that is what I would throw on when I was just out of the shower, doing my hair and makeup. I would literally stand in my closet in my kimono, looking at the rows and rows of options thinking, *Ohmigod, I have nothing to wear.* I would then begin the clothes-trying-on ceremony by looking at the row of size-2 pants that I couldn't get over my thighs since having my daughter. I would lovingly gaze at them and occasionally even try to put a pair on after slaving away at the gym. The result was always the same: suck in the tummy, hold my breath, and pull. My favorite jeans, size 2, would slide over my ankles, past my calves, over my knees and…done. There was no possible way I was ever getting those, not to mention many other items in my closet, back into the normal rotation of wearable items.

I actually liked the curves that I earned carrying my daughter, and I had lost almost all of the seventy pounds of baby weight I had gained during my pregnancy with the help of a trainer. (And I do realize that a pregnancy gain of seventy pounds is a bit excessive, but I gave in to every whim and craving when I was pregnant, and as a thirty-five-year-old thrilled with being pregnant for the first time, I indulged.) My body just wasn't shaped the same way. So why was I keeping all of these items? I was confident in my body, and I wasn't someone who body shamed herself or obsessed over what size she was. I was healthy and strong, and I felt good in my skin.

I dove into research about emotional attachment to items. What I found was that most people attach memories to items, and those memories have a tendency to spark an emotional response. This was the reason that my jeans (that were too small) were still hanging in my closet. I definitely knew that, regardless of how much time I spent in the gym or what diet I put myself on, it was highly unlikely that the activity was going to yield the type of results that would get those jeans over my hips. And truth be told, I actually didn't even want to be that size again, so it wasn't going to happen.

I finally had enough of my closet winning what I can only describe as a never-ending chess match that I was always losing. I marked off a day on my calendar as "doomsday" and set a reminder in my phone to keep me focused. I was going to simplify my closet.

When doomsday arrived, I went through my closet and got rid of every item of clothing that didn't fit. It was liberating to decide that I would not allow myself to be emotionally attached to anything that did not have value. That dress that was two sizes too small and had a retail value of $400 a few years prior had a value of zero if I couldn't wear it. The process of going through all the items in my closet and filling those donation bags with pieces that I had once really enjoyed was one of the best feelings. I experienced great joy getting rid of the expectations that I had unknowingly set for myself by keeping those items. I cleaned out half of the items in my closet that day—a collection of clothing that was the wrong size, ill fitting, or not worthy of being among the well-tailored, quality items that I enjoyed wearing on a daily basis.

If you have things that you are keeping but not using because "maybe, one day" you may want to wear them or use them, get rid of them. Donate them or throw them out. Simplify your choices, and your life will immediately feel more cohesive. The act of de-cluttering needs to be done before you ever start to organize what you will keep. Both actions help de-clutter your life, but organizing without decluttering first simply moves the clutter around. The first step should always be decluttering actually getting rid of the stuff you don't use regularly or love. And only after thoroughly decluttering should you think about organizing to further simplify your life.

If you have an item of clothing that makes you feel bad when you put it on, get rid of it. The simple act of taking back your happiness by not subjecting yourself to the standards of the past will give you happiness. If you value living in the moment and maximizing your potential, you have to start looking at daily routines and change any routine that doesn't contribute to feelings of joy.

This solution may seem simple, but as you start going through your stuff, memories of events, people, and situations will come flooding back to you, creating an emotional connection to these items. Don't fall into the trap! If you were given one week to live, how would you spend it? Would you sit in your home, clutching your favorite pair of pants that you haven't worn since 1999, or would you finally start to live your life?

I look at life completely differently than I did ten years ago. Time has become more valuable than things, and I have become extremely aware of the fact that, as you age, you are exactly the same but wiser. I feel the same way I did twenty years ago, but my body has aged. I am fully aware that who I am is not only this body; my body is just the vessel that holds my soul here on earth.

ACCOUNTABILITY STEP

What are some things you can do to simplify your life and daily routine? Write down three things you can change today that will help you simplify your daily routine.

CHAPTER 14

CONFIDENCE IS YOUR SUPERPOWER

I have always liked magazines. When I was young, my mother would allow my siblings and me to pick out candy when we went to the grocery store. I always begged for a magazine instead. I enjoyed looking at the pictures of all the beautiful, perfect people. I daydreamed about all the exotic places I would visit when I grew up. As I got older, my friends all talked about what celebrities where doing and wearing. I became aware at a very early age that people seemed to be more concerned with what other people were doing than they were with what they themselves were doing. I followed all the trends and watched all the celebrities just as everyone else did until I was about thirty, when I started realizing that I should focus some energy into my own life.

Have you ever looked in the mirror and thought to yourself, "Wow, I look amazing!" If you have, congratulations on taking the first step in deprogramming your brain and erasing the propaganda that you may have been exposed to by the media or on television. Most of the images (branding) that we see are images of people who have been retouched or flat-out manipulated to market a product (for example, the exaggerated thigh gap). These manipulated images are unfortunately setting unrealistic expectations not only for women but also for men. Our brain is constantly processing information, and these manipulated images become hardwired in our brain if we allow our worth to be determined by the liar in the mirror.

When we look into the mirror, we see a reflection of what our brain tells us we look like. What most of us do not stop to think about is the fact that the reflection we see is only a perception. What if I told you that what you see in the mirror is not what other people see? I am definitely not suggesting that the reflection is not you, or that what you see is not close to what others see, but what I can tell you is that when you look in the mirror, whatever you notice first is not going to be what someone else notices first.

We are all unique, but so many people I know strive to look like other people. I have definitely embraced the concept of becoming the best me I can be. I am focused on trying to be healthy and working on personal growth so that my inner beauty is just as stunning as my outer beauty. I am not perfect, and some will say I am not beautiful or even pretty, but I am me and that is all I can be. I am beautiful and kind. I am smart and giving. I am joyful and reflective. I am just like you. We all have different outer shells, but inside we are all the same. We all want to love and be loved, and that, my friends, is what you should see when you look in the mirror. That mirror may try to tell you that your neck is fat or your nose is big, but you tell that mirror that it is a liar. We are all unique; why do we compare ourselves to unrealistic expectations?

Escapism is real, and so many people I know dive into other people's lives instead of concentrating on their own. What would happen if you took all the energy that you're spending comparing your life to someone else's and just worked on your own personal growth? I can tell you what would happen: you would more quickly discover your purpose. Instead of watching sitcoms and documentaries about other people's lives, you would start living your own. We have to practice and embrace self-love and stop criticizing ourselves. When and how did we all become our own worst critics?

The quality of our relationships is also determined by the way we feel about ourselves and what we see when we look in the mirror. We are meant to live in our full potential, and when we do so, we allow our relationships to be the fullest that they can be as well. The universe lines us up with experiences that will allow us to make new choices and break out of old patterns, which is a deeply liberating experience and one in which we discover our power and connection with the loving force within us and around us—the one that is constantly nudging and guiding us to our right thoughts, our right actions, and our right choices.

Our habit is to focus on what's not working on the outside and try to fix it. I encourage you to shift your attention to what's happening on the inside and deepen your attention on and awareness of your inner life. When we focus on our internal space and take care of that first, everything on the outside lines up. Our internal landscape is made up not only of our physical body but also our thoughts and emotions.

Spend some peaceful time alone each day where you can meditate, journal, do something you love, and connect with yourself. Give yourself this space to release anything that is no longer serving you—thoughts, worries, or emotions. Many people think that our purpose should be obvious and easy to identify, a notion that leads to much frustration and disappointment. More often, your purpose will slowly emerge as you put one foot in front of the other, following where your heart, talents, and life overall seem to be leading you.

When we connect with who we really are from a place of enlightenment, we have the capacity to magnetize to us our desires and experience relationships and a life that is fulfilling, happy, and loving. This will help you to realize your actual purpose. You have to know who you are and love that person before the process of finding your purpose becomes easier. Some people spend years trying to define their purpose because they haven't yet learned the art of self-discovery.

Self-discovery requires that you dig deep even back to your childhood to start looking at the experiences, both good and bad, that shaped who you are. It is the analysis of your core beliefs and making a commitment to live by them. The path of self-discovery will lead you to your purpose.

Wikipedia defines self-discovery as:

"…a travel, pilgrimage, or series of events whereby a person attempts to determine how they feel, personally, about spiritual issues or priorities, rather than following the opinions of family, friends, neighborhood, or peer pressure. The topic of self-discovery has been associated with Zen. A related term is 'finding oneself.'"

In my opinion, Wikipedia hit the nail on the head. When you journey on a path of self-discovery, you determine exactly who you are. When you know who you are, it is easier to identify your path of purpose.

There are ten actions that have helped me discover my inner self and purpose, and these actionable steps will help you to get there as well.

Positive Daily Affirmations

Habits are behaviors that are performed automatically because they have been performed frequently in the past. This repetition creates a mental association between the situation (cue) and the action (behavior), which means that when the cue is encountered, the behavior is performed automatically. Automatic actions have a number of components, one of which is lack of thought.

Train Your Brain with Positive Self-Talk

As with any new skill, training your brain to think differently takes time. But the more you practice thinking positively, the more mental muscle you'll build. In addition, your brain will undergo physical changes that will permanently help you think differently.

Be Accountable and Make a Gratitude List

While in a grateful mood, we will feel gratitude more frequently, and when we do feel gratitude, it will be more intense and last longer. We will feel gratitude for more things at the same time. Gratitude triggers positive feedback loops.

Stay Away from Life Leeches

Negative people in your life will have a negative effect on your life. Audit your inner circle regularly and do not subscribe to the limits that other people voice. You are the author of your own life, so surround yourself with winners if you want to win.

Stop Being a Victim

A victim mentality will only keep you living in victim circumstances. Stop playing the blame game and move on. Life will kick you when you are down, but you have to rise above. The most important thing you can do is to look at your life as a journey to greatness. The only limits we have are the limits we place on ourselves.

Create that Vision Board

What we focus on expands. When you create a vision board and place it in a space where you see it often, you essentially end up doing short visualization exercises throughout the day. Those exercises help direct energy toward your goal.

Eliminate Self-Doubt and Trust Your Intuition

Learn to trust yourself. The power of trusting your intuition has been embraced by successful executive management teams and favored by successful individuals such as Steve Jobs, who said, "Intuition is a very powerful thing, more powerful than intellect, in my opinion. That's had a big impact on my work."

Stop Living in the Past

The past is gone. Dwelling on the past can make you lose sight of your present life. This can make your life quickly pass you by without enjoyment of the present.

Choose Happiness

Happiness is a choice and an action. Remember, "Happiness is my choice." Most of us have been conditioned to believe that happiness is an indulgence, when in fact, it is merely an action. When you choose happiness and take action to be happy, you will experience happiness.

Stop Chasing

If you are chasing anything or otherwise forcing something that is not meant to be, you are cheating yourself out of experiencing the greatness that the world has for you. If you are busy chasing love from someone who doesn't love you, you will miss the person who does love you. We tell ourselves the lie that, one day, maybe they'll realize and reciprocate our intentions, but they rarely do, and all of the effort and energy that we invested leaves us with nothing but wasted time and heartache.

If you chase success only to gain financial wealth, you will have a pile of money and a pile of problems to go along with it. If you stop chasing and allow energy to flow freely into the universe and align yourself with success and love, your life will be limitless. Go after what you want in life but take accountability for your choices and create a plan so you are not doomed to the constant chase.

ACCOUNTABILITY STEP

Ask yourself: "Am I taking a strategic approach to life, or am I just chasing?" Write down three reasons that have been persuading you not to go for your big dream. Across from each, write out the worst-case scenario if they came true. Are the worst-case scenarios really that bad?

CHAPTER FIFTEEN

CUPID'S ARROW

C an we talk for just a minute above love? Love is one of the fundamental "things" we all want and some people chase, but what are we doing to attract the right type of love?

Who we are and how much we love ourselves has an enormous impact on the people who are drawn into our lives. We attract what we are, so if you are a single person who has a positive outlook on life and who lives a life that revolves around embracing the greater good, you are going to attract the same type of people.

Right now, as I am writing this chapter, I am a single woman. It is a jungle out there, ladies and gentlemen, there's no doubt about it. But I believe that love not only exists but thrives in our communities. That said, with the abundance of dating apps to choose from and a culture that is looking for instant gratification, how do we find life-long partners who are like-minded? We have become so guarded with our feelings that, as a society, I often wonder if we have disconnected from the notion of deep meaningful relationships.

I would love to remarry, but it would have to be to a true life partner, someone who truly seeks the greater good and wants to live on a path of constant personal and professional growth. It is not easy being a single mother with a demanding career, but it is far easier than settling into a life in which I was not designed to flourish and grow.

With the explosion of dating apps creating a swipe left, swipe right society, where is the romance and organic connection that makes our hearts skip a beat? No matter what we tell ourselves, we all want the same thing: a real, authentic, raw connection that makes modern dating and instant gratification seem foolish.

After my divorce, I spent a few years focused solely on my career and my daughter. When I decided to dip my toe into the dating pool, I discovered that technology had replaced actual face-to-face interactions. I decided to embrace innovation and took the plunge by creating an online profile. I had my profile up for exactly thirty days before I realized that this was not the approach for me. I have so many friends who have found love on Match and eHarmony, but I had a hard time trying to navigate through the BS to find any authentic connections.

If you haven't been on an online dating site, let me explain how this all goes down. You post a profile and start getting hundreds of messages from prospective suitors wanting to connect (in one way or another). It is overwhelming at best, and it requires a huge time commitment to properly sort through the comments, delete the creepers, cross-check the nice messages to profiles and narrow down the list to some actually viable candidates. I tried to make time to engage, but as a busy woman raising a daughter, I just couldn't invest the time needed to forge into the jungle and find the gold hidden in a vast forestry of as-yet uncharted territory. I wanted to make an authentic connection, but I kept running into messages that read, "Hi cutie, want to connect?" Gross.

I went on a few dates with men who had posted a profile pic from at least ten years prior, and I didn't feel a true connection with anyone. There was one guy I met who seemed promising, but after a few dates I realized he just wasn't the right match for me.

I gave up on online dating after thirty days, but I have never given up on love. I have been in love a few times in my life, and I know what it feels like and how wonderful it can be. I have been in one-sided relationships and lackluster relationships, but every-one who has been in my life has served a purpose. I either learned a life lesson or I discovered something about myself that I didn't previously know.

One of the most valuable things that I have learned about love is that it will happen when it is supposed to happen if you put yourself in its path. The love that you are meant to have in your life is not represented by someone who you have to chase or convince to love you. So many people, myself included, have tried to convince someone to love them; that is nothing more than a waste of your time. The worst possible thing that you can do is go against the natural flow of attraction and authentic connection. We are biologically designed to connect with certain people. The people with whom we have a strong biological connection are the people who take our breath away. There will be physical attraction to people on a superficial sexual-attraction level, but true love is different. You can have an intense feeling of affection for someone, which means that you view someone as awesome and desirable based on your beliefs, judgments, and experiences. Once you decide that someone is attractive mentally and physically, love also becomes a biological process. Your body takes over and reinforces what your mind already knows: this person makes you feel amazing!

The physical reaction to love is a neurological condition whereby we feel bonded to something or someone else. When we feel this kind of attachment, our brain releases hormones such as serotonin, oxytocin, vasopressin, dopamine, and norepinephrine. All of these cause us to think loving thoughts and feel the physical sensations that we associate with love. The SOVDN of love is defined as:

Serotonin

This hormone increases your mood. It is also associated with the status aspect of love and the "idea" of love.

Oxytocin

This hormone has been referred to as the biological basis for love. It is released during cuddling and sex, and it helps to give you the feeling of attachment to someone else.

Vasopressin

Along with oxytocin, experts believe that this hormone causes one to feel attached to someone.

Dopamine

This hormone is responsible for desire and reward, which means you feel an immense amount of pleasure when you are rewarded with loving actions, such as kindness, touch, date night, or whatever makes you feel fulfilled and happy.

Norepinephrine

Norepinephrine is released when you are falling in love and feel stress for things to work out and go well. It gives you the physical sensations you feel while falling in love, such as sweaty palms or a racing heart.

In other words, among many other things, hormones regulate our behavior as we are falling in love. Does the fact that the feelings of love are part of a hormonal process make love not as impactful as we think? Not at all. The feeling of love is a powerful emotion that benefits us in a big way.

Love can inspire, motivate, and empower. You have the ability within yourself to use your intuition as a guide to determine who is right for your life. You have heard people use the term "red flags" when they are dating potential life partners, and all of us know what our non-negotiable terms are. Trust your natural intuition when it comes to bringing people into your life, and only surround yourself with supportive people who are going to lift you up.

We are designed to be social creatures, but being in a relationship might not be beneficial for you or your partner if you need to work on yourself first. We all go through self-reflection, and if you have a supportive partner in your life, those periods have the ability to allow both people to grow together as one. Friendships that are driven more by a pre-existing similarity rather than friends who become more similar over time due to influencing each other will end in a more compatible relationship. We are sometimes drawn to the passion behind the notion that "opposites attract," but the reality is that while passion may be great for the bedroom, it can be disastrous everywhere else.

Don't settle for average if you are a single person who wants to be in a relationship. Find things that you are passionate about, and use those activities to meet other like-minded people. You will draw the right people into your life just by being the real you. You want to attract people into your life who love you for who you authentically are, without filters.

Success is all about confidence, but so is attracting love. Be confident in who you are and what your belief system is. So many people settle for a life partner who isn't going to help them build a mutually beneficial life simply because they do not want to end up "alone." Alone is a state of mind and a victim mentality. You are never alone if you are engaging with other people and concentrating on building the life you want for yourself. While I still love the idea of marriage, I am not going to put my life on hold until I meet the person who will be the king to my queen status.

The last thing I have to say about love is that the decisions that you make regarding intimate relationships in your life will influence everything about the quality of your life. Trust is paramount.

Never waste your time with anyone you are hoping to "change," regardless of the chemistry between you. It is narcissistic to want them to change and ignorant to expect them to. Look to have a relationship with people who you respect, admire, and enjoy just as they are now or doom yourself to settling for a life that you were not intended to live. Life is beautiful and amazing, with so many twists and turns that you can celebrate with your partner. Your daily environment will have a direct impact on the quality of your life.

If you are dating someone who is constantly struggling with trusting you or is even so bold to tell you that they don't want you to look at their phone, run. The habit of someone turning a phone upside down so the screen isn't exposed is a big flashing red flag- pay attention. If you are married to someone who isn't supportive or doesn't add value to your life, communicate that! I would never recommend that someone leave their marriage unless their happiness is being destroyed. With counseling and clear, deliberate communication, some marriages can be rehabilitated into relationships that create deep and lasting happiness. Some cannot. Trust your intuition and instincts. If you think your partner has something to hide, they probably do. True love is trusting, kind, and supportive. Do not waste any of your time on someone who is not. Trust me, your life deserves happiness, and you're worth it.

ACCOUNTABILITY STEPS

The best way to attract "The One" into your life is to become the best version of yourself. Be confident and look for friendship first. Write down your deal breakers and stick to them. Only you know what is best for your own life.

CHAPTER 16

LIVE YOUR BEST LIFE

The truth isn't always rainbows and unicorns, and as a practicing member of the positivity club, the reality still is that life is hard. I love life, but it isn't always a walk in the park. What separates the victims from the warriors in this world is accountability. You can implement techniques for personal and professional development, you can take courses and invest in coaching from some of the top executive coaches and motivators in the world, but if you do not follow up with accountability, you are putting yourself at risk for living life as a victim. Make no mistake, accountability is hard, and requires humility. You cannot achieve any worthwhile personal or professional goal if you don't hold yourself accountable. The reason is simple: it's your life! If you have to be held accountable at work, don't expect to be promoted or to experience any type of significant career advancement. If you have to be held accountable at home by your parents, roommate, or spouse, it will grow old fast and your relationships will deteriorate. Holding yourself accountable is nothing more than following through with YOUR commitments and responsibilities. It's doing what YOU know you should do, WHEN you should do it,

It may sound easy enough to implement yourself, but many people need to hire an accountability coach to hold them accountable to living their best life. Everyone's personality is different, which is the most important thing I have learned from working with clients in accountability. Some clients come to me for three months of coaching, and some come for twelve. Each one of us if we are honest with ourselves can identify our own weaknesses. It shows strength and courage not to let them hold you back. When you take 100 percent responsibility for embracing accountability, your performance will improve, your relationships will flourish, your market value will soar, people's respect for you will skyrocket, you will be a great example for others to follow, and your self-esteem will grow.

In all of these areas of your life, you can see such dramatic improvement. When you hold yourself accountable to doing the things you know you should do, you will distinguish yourself from the crowd. This is your life! Starting right now, commit to being the best version of yourself, and never look back. You deserve it, and so does everyone around you. Walk in your power. There is only one of you in this world, and you were meant for great things. In this world you have to make a choice. You can live the life of a victim or become a survivor training to be a warrior. I have so much love for each of you, and I hope that you choose to #EmbraceAccountability and live your best life.

ACKNOWLEDGEMENTS

I want to start out by expressing gratitude to everyone who has been a part of my journey so far to get me to where I am today. I am so thankful for all of my experiences. I want all of you to know that, without you, I wouldn't be where I am today, so I thank each of you. I wish you nothing but a life of happiness.

I would like to thank the people who have influenced my life. Brené Brown, Tony Robbins, Gary Vaynerchuk, and Grant and Elena Cardone have each inspired me to publish this book. Thank you, Lisa C. Copeland, for your friendship and support, and for introducing me to my fabulous editor, Elizabeth Lyons. If one person reads this book and decides to stop settling for average, it is a success and has served its purpose.

To my daughter, Isabella, you have inspired me to be everything that I have become, and you have given me the gift of gratitude. I love you more than words can ever express, and your life is going to be so full of happiness. You are the greatest gift in my life.

Thank you to the many friends I have had during different seasons of my life. Every one of you has been critical to my growth, and I've learned so much from each of you. If I try to name you all, I will definitely leave someone out, so I am going to leave it as "you know who you are," and I appreciate you. Empowerment starts with you realizing your own worth and a special thank you goes out to everyone who inspired me to realize mine. You are the reason that my passion burns so brightly to help others. I love each of you.

ABOUT THE AUTHOR

Melissa Burrow is a mother, advocate, and ambitious goal slayer who has spent over twenty years in the male-dominated automotive industry, serving in management and executive leadership roles. Recognized as a dynamic, innovative thought leader and industry expert, she is passionate about changing the culture of businesses both inside and outside the automotive industry to create leaders who embrace accountability and foster positive, productive work environments. Her belief that everyone deserves to live their best life combined with her passion for personal development and servant leadership inspired her to become an accountability coach to help others create strategic action plans to achieve their goals.

Melissa lives in Texas with her brilliant daughter, her camera-obsessed cat, Penelope, and her eleven-year-old Yorkie, The Great Gatsby.

Instagram: @iammelissaburrow
Facebook: Facebook.com/melissalburrow
Twitter: @MelissaLBurrow